Home Sweet Glass Home

Written by
Kimberly T. Suders

In consultation with Dr. D. Neil Suders

Many Blessings!

Kimberly T. Sudius

Romans 12

This book is written as my offering of praise and honor to God. Without God, there would be no writing of it. It is written in dedication to my remarkable husband, Dr. D. Neil Suders, and with my love and appreciation for the priceless inspiration given to me by my amazing son, daughter, and granddaughter. Thank you for being my most valuable treasures!

Contents

Introduction: Blueprints ix

Called 13

It's Personal. 16

Authentic Leaders 20

Fraud Protection 28

The Glass House 37

Foundation Blocks 41

Full Disclosure 54

Home Repairs 58

Fixer-upper 63

The Un-welcome Mat 67

Spring Cleaning 71

Neighbors 74

Neighborhood Watch 80

A House Divided. 83

House Fire. 87

Without Power 91

New Paint 96

Curb Appeal 102

Growing Pains. 106

Septic Tank 111

Windowpanes 118

Home Sweet Glass Home 121

Introduction: Blueprints

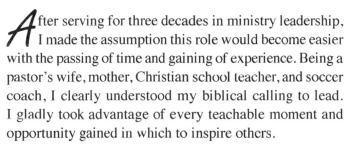

*A*fter serving for three decades in ministry leadership, I made the assumption this role would become easier with the passing of time and gaining of experience. Being a pastor's wife, mother, Christian school teacher, and soccer coach, I clearly understood my biblical calling to lead. I gladly took advantage of every teachable moment and opportunity gained in which to inspire others.

Upon returning home after a day of teaching high school Bible classes, I found myself frustrated, angry, and deeply disappointed. I pleaded with God: Why did my students seem so apathetic and unmoved as we studied and read His precious Word, day after day? Tears fell as I prayed. I failed to determine a reason for my students' indifference.

I applied every creative method of teaching and used every available resource, yet most students continued to resist a committed relationship with Jesus Christ. I asked God: After all this time, why is leadership still so difficult instead of becoming easier?

Adding to my discouragement, the anxiety caused by the constant demands of church leadership overwhelmed me. I felt as though my every word and action were scrutinized, assessed, and criticized for perfection. In comparison, I likened myself to one living in a completely transparent *glass house*. It seemed no aspect of my life remained personal and private.

I became concerned and distraught, since bitterness replaced the joy of ministry which once consumed my heart. In my brokenness, I recognized who was to blame: myself, the leader. In God's exposure of my failures and inadequacies as a leader, He made it clear I must accept full responsibility for the indifference of my followers, due to my lack of God-centered, effective leadership.

My incorrect perceptions of leadership were negative, defensive, and authoritative. After all, I established them for myself based upon my desires and the examples I had witnessed from other leaders. My belief was people should follow me, just because I said so. It never occurred to me, but the scrutiny of my *glass house* life is God's intended tool for use in my leadership ministry.

We leaders are granted many opportunities in which to make choices. We may choose an aggressive, superior, and self-exalting approach to leadership, or we may choose the approach characterized by integrity, sincerity, and transparency. We may choose to accept a lifetime of leadership, while dwelling in a figurative glass house, or we may reject a personal, vulnerable connection to our followers.

In ministry today, I am deeply concerned. We leaders are not leading in ways that motivate and inspire others to become successful in and dedicated to Christ. We Christians appear to have relationships with Christ that are no longer spiritually committed, but are socially convenient. I believe I must accept responsibility, define godly leadership, and use the platform provided by my *glass house* to make a difference in the lives of people today.

Leader, will you join with me in my resolution to offer godly, effective leadership in the Body of Christ? Will you share my passion to be an inspirational, righteous leader, governed by integrity, sincerity, and transparency? Along with me, will you make necessary changes in order to guide followers to a productive relationship with God? Will you be willing to accept God's mandate to live in a *glass house* as an example for others? Through these commitments, we can impact the world and make a difference by way of our leadership!

Called

*A*t the time of writing this book, my husband, Neil, and I have been in ministry for over thirty years. It amazes me to look back over those years and remember; we began when I was just a mere nineteen years old. We were not yet married, but we worked side by side in volunteer youth ministry. We were completing our degrees of higher learning from Liberty University, Neil's degree in Pastoral and Youth Ministries, mine in English and Communications. Our dream was to graduate, marry, have a family, and inspire countless others with the Gospel of Jesus Christ. For certain, God called us to full-time ministry, and we had it in our minds; we would be good at it. Oh, to be so young, romantic, and foolishly misguided! Through the years, God has educated us far beyond classroom training and our hearts' passions. It took some time and experience for us to understand what it truly means to be *called of God* and to be ministers and servants of the Lord.

In today's culture of the church or ministry, many descriptions and titles are given to those who are called to lead. There may be the Senior Pastor. The youth pastor may be the Pastor of Youth and Student Ministries. Someone, once called a children's pastor, may now be a team of multi-leadership composed of a Director of Preschool Ministries, Primary Children's Coordinator, and Pastor of Intermediate Students. Titles for all ministry leadership come in many different forms, with very different areas of focus, and great expectations.

Ministries and organizations today support a staff of few or a staff of many. There are part-time positions and full-time positions. There may be associate pastors for discipleship, administration, care-giving, and visitation. The small group approach to discipleship has proven quite effective, so there are often coordinators, facilitators, and hosts for this ministry. Some churches and organizations establish Christian schools or seminaries as part of their outreach. In this arena, there are leaders who serve in the academic setting as professors, teachers, coaches, and administrators. Because God calls leaders to specific ministries, He equips us with specific strengths and abilities to accomplish leading for His glory.

Ministries also enlist a support staff of volunteers or lay-leaders. These dear people give freely of their time to teach classes, provide nursery care, coordinate the technology, or direct choirs. These volunteers frequently facilitate major workings of a Sunday morning worship service, serving as ushers, musicians, vocalists, or housekeepers. They may serve as elders or deacons. The areas of service available for the lay-leaders are numerable. These saints are also equipped with gifts from the Lord, so they may offer positive assistance in accomplishing the work of the ministry. They, in turn, are called as lay-leaders.

When we are called by God to become one of His children by redemption through His Son, Jesus Christ, we are given many opportunities to lead others in some capacity. These leadership roles may be large or small, well-known or little known, frequent or periodical, continual, or for a determined season. Regardless of specific titles and positions, we are chosen leaders. With a leadership role comes great responsibility, accountability, and capability. We must be an example to the Body of Christ and an inspiration to those who do not yet know Him as their Savior.

Because God calls us to leadership, He offers us the privilege to assist Him in His kingdom work, whether it is in the church, mission work, education, our community, or business.

It's Personal!

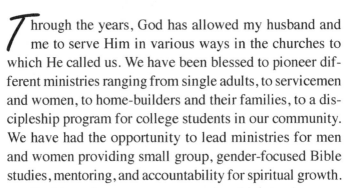

*T*hrough the years, God has allowed my husband and me to serve Him in various ways in the churches to which He called us. We have been blessed to pioneer different ministries ranging from single adults, to servicemen and women, to home-builders and their families, to a discipleship program for college students in our community. We have had the opportunity to lead ministries for men and women providing small group, gender-focused Bible studies, mentoring, and accountability for spiritual growth.

God has given us many ways in which to share our experiences and higher learning to teach workshops for leaders, church staff, and lay-workers. In addition, God has given my husband opportunities to teach in biblical institute and college settings. We have also been given platforms by which to share our remarkable blessings and guidance of the Lord at retreats, banquets, camps, and spiritual rallies.

Regardless of so many God-given venues in which to share our faith in Him, the majority of our years in ministry have been spent in the youth or senior pastorate. In spite of the fact that monetary compensation was not always possible for some churches for their pastors, God always provided what we needed. At times, it was necessary for us to maintain employment in the job market while remaining committed to our pastoral leadership ministry. The Lord requires that we offer ourselves to Him regardless of the compensation we might receive. He is our reward! His blessings upon our lives have allowed us to serve freely and uninhibited to those to whom He sends us. Because His blessings are so abundant, we have always had a home in which to live and food on our table. Monthly bills have always been paid, and financial obligations have always been fulfilled. There is no need to worry when God calls us to be His leaders.

I think of the countless times that God has blessed us so others could see His mighty work. It was remarkable to see my husband, Neil, work very diligently as he was senior pastor to a congregation, completed two Master's degrees programs, and completed an academic program with a full dissertation to receive his Doctorate of Ministries. The focus and endurance with which the Lord sustained Neil was remarkable! Those who witnessed this were overwhelmed to see the power of the Lord working, without limitations, in the life of someone they knew.

Neil never missed a step as far as our flock of sheep was concerned. He preached the Word of God through the power of the Holy Spirit every Sunday. Even while studying to accomplish the educational requirements, he never compromised the quality and quantity of the time needed to study the Word of God in preparation for each sermon. He led in discipleship groups, participated in the music ministry, conducted weddings and funerals, and attended the sporting and special events of the students in our church, just to name a few.

All the while, we continued to grow in our relationship with one another in our marriage. After all, marriage is a never-ending, disciplined, unselfish process that rewards and enriches the couple who continues to invest in it. This is no exception for a leader and his or her spouse. God gave me my husband, a precious gift, and He permits me to serve by Neil's side every step of the way. Talk about a place of blessing! After many years, I happily remain in this place.

While I am called to follow the leadership of my husband I am, first and foremost, called to follow Christ. In obedience to my calling, I am to serve the Lord, honor my husband, and lead my children to follow and obey God. I am also called to lead, so that I might inspire others. I am called to be an example and to lead in spite of the opinions of others. I am called to lead, whether I win or lose. I am called to lead, so I will never forget the meaning of being a great follower. I am called to lead in order to know God and His Word better than I know myself. I am called to lead, so I may choose to hide in the background, allowing others to be successful and noticed in the fore-front. I am called to lead in spite of my faults. I am called to think less of myself, more of others, and the most of God. I am called to lead, so others see that God is Truth. I **am called** to lead!

Since God leads us, helping us to obey His calling and lead others, He has always been faithful to provide the practical necessities as well as the spiritual sustenance for us to serve Him and the Body of Christ. God gives us the boldness, the discretion, the compassion, the firmness, the sensitivity, and the resilience to serve Him and

His children, anywhere and in any capacity. He gives us the opportunities to establish relationships with those we lead while He continues to strengthen His relationship with each and every one of us, personally. Since God distinctly chooses us, we must recognize, with all seriousness and sincerity, the weight of His call. **He** makes us into **His** own personal leaders.

Authentic Leaders

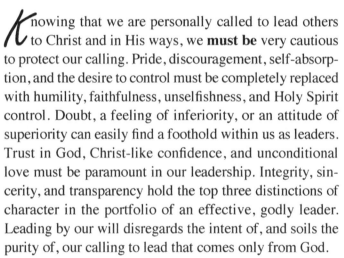

*K*nowing that we are personally called to lead others to Christ and in His ways, we **must be** very cautious to protect our calling. Pride, discouragement, self-absorption, and the desire to control must be completely replaced with humility, faithfulness, unselfishness, and Holy Spirit control. Doubt, a feeling of inferiority, or an attitude of superiority can easily find a foothold within us as leaders. Trust in God, Christ-like confidence, and unconditional love must be paramount in our leadership. Integrity, sincerity, and transparency hold the top three distinctions of character in the portfolio of an effective, godly leader. Leading by our will disregards the intent of, and soils the purity of, our calling to lead that comes only from God.

Because we are leaders, we must be continuously aware of our personal and spiritual weaknesses which can spiral us downward into a strong-willed, hostile, and fleshly leader almost instantaneously. We must never forget our greatest strengths can also be our greatest weaknesses when the wrong motivation drives them. No matter how honorable our intentions, self-or-sin-driven leadership is wrong. As godly leaders, we cannot feign that we are something we are not. We must be absolutely authentic in spite of our wonderful strengths and terrible weaknesses.

The first step in proving our authenticity as leaders is to appreciate our attributes, yet humbly admit our weaknesses. It is likely we as leaders called by God share many similar, good qualities. As genes are passed from one generation to the next within a family, so weaknesses are passed through the generations of sinful mankind. Because we are within the family of God, we leaders may share similar challenges and struggles. Authenticity displays our fortitude to attack our weaknesses with force, making minimal or completely destroying them. Weaknesses pose the greatest threat to us as authentic leaders. It is imperative; we must recognize them and set a course of action to exterminate them.

WEAKNESS WARNING: **Discouragement.** Being human, we feel pain. Circumstances and people can hurt us; Satan will definitely hurt us. As authentic leaders, we must admit our pain. We leaders may become discouraged, since Satan is intending that our outlook is negative and not positive. We are not invincible, but we can be immovable. Remember, dear one; God filters the pain that comes upon us through His own omnipotent hands. The pain comes, but it will not keep us down. God will not permit it. Do not be discouraged; all is not lost. Our victory just has not yet been won!

Leaders must not deny the fact that discouragement will come, but we must deny that it will keep its hold on us. Authentic leaders admit our attacks from discouragement, but we must claim victory. God will not allow us to be overtaken by it. We must not say, "Woe is me;" but, "Woe, to the cause of discouragement!" As an example to our followers, our faith must clearly be seen. God is forever faithful to give us victory. Leaders are to be faithful in proving that God gives us victory because of our faith in Him. We are faithful; God is faithful. God is faithful; we are faithful. This weaving completely covers discouragement.

WEAKNESS WARNING: **Self-absorption.** Guarding against self-absorption seems like an obvious caution to us as authentic leaders. After all, it is abnormal to go through our day telling everyone we see, *"Everything is all about me!"* Since this behavior seems so extremely peculiar for any leader, we must be very aware of how it appears and affects us. Self-absorption might be seen in our attitude following a time of discouragement. It might be seen if we leaders feel we are being unduly criticized by others. In this case, we see ourselves as the victims of another's attacks.

Self-absorption might be seen through the best of intentions. As leaders, we become so busy and over-loaded with the work of leadership, we lose focus on the heart of the ministry in the first place. We fail to maintain our priorities properly, such as our personal heart-to-heart relationships with God, our spouses, or our families. We become so absorbed in doing everything ourselves — micro-managing every task, making all decisions, adding more items to that figurative plate — we become completely self-absorbed, hoping everyone else can see what we are capable of doing. We must remember; the heavier this plate becomes, the more we will be unable to hold it firmly, not to mention spilling it and making a complete mess of everything! Self-absorption is completely focused on us, the leaders, and never allows us to look beyond ourselves.

As self-absorbed leaders, we label ourselves with the big name tag: *selfish*. In battle, leaders lead the way. When playing the game of Follow the Leader, the leader goes first. Having others align themselves in a line behind a leader implies the leader is in the front of the line. If we are **not** selfish and self-absorbed leaders, we understand; in battle, we may be the first to fall. For others to follow, we may have to first *get down and dirty ourselves*, so they will. For others to align themselves behind us, we leaders must be in the correct place, so the followers can see where we intend to lead them. Leading is always about others and never about us.

WEAKNESS WARNING: **Stubborn Control.** As authentic leaders, we must recognize that we have been given the authority to lead, but we are not the final authority. A stubborn desire to control everything and everyone will cause inappropriate conflicts within our ministry. I say "inappropriate conflicts" because this battle comes from our improper perspective as leaders. It is a "my way or the highway" attitude. The leader who continually reminds others, "I am in charge," has lost sight of God's perspective for His leaders. Such a leader believes that we routinely face opposition from followers. We constantly have a fight to fight. In this, we pervert the definition of "fighting the **good** fight."

We leaders must be confident in the things that we have seen God accomplish, but we must not be controlling, thinking that we can accomplish things in place of God. If we become controlling leaders, we can never enable others to reach their full potential for Christ. We will be constantly combative, looking to criticize, ultimately becoming pros-ecutor, judge, and jury. A stubborn, controlling leader will not admit faults, failures, and wrong-doings. We will be filled with anger and hostility towards others.

We can never model true repentance before those who follow us if our desire is to control, control, and control more! For something or someone to be controlled, there must be a controller.

As leaders, who is our controller? Without a doubt, the Holy Spirit is to be the One who controls every step and every aspect of our leadership. He is **in** us, so He can work **through** us.

WEAKNESS WARNING: **Doubt.** Who of us leaders has never doubted? The authentic leader admits his struggle with doubt. Throughout our time of leadership, we see God's greatness and answers to prayer; however, there are times when it appears as though God is sitting silent, as if He has not heard anything we have prayed. While assuming not much is happening and things are not happening quickly enough, doubt creeps in on us.

It is easy for leaders to think that God might halt His working in our lives. In particular, if we see our followers become complacent or apathetic about passionately fol-lowing the Lord, we doubt that He is working through us, the leaders, any longer. We may have experienced our chil-dren or family members falling away from God, and we doubt that we have led them as God intends. It may seem we are wandering in a spiritual wilderness where God told us to go in the first place; yet, He seems to be apart from us. Doubt simply freezes us leaders in our tracks and causes us to stop leading, even for just one step.

Remember, dear leader; God's Word is still telling us the way in which to lead. We must turn our eyes to it. God promises He will care for every part of our lives **if** we trust Him. As we trusted in our parents when we were children, we were certain that they would love us, protect us, and provide for us. We doubted their good judgment at times, but our trust in them far out-weighed our doubt. Remember the old hymn, "Trust and Obey"? One verse states: "Not a **doubt** nor a fear; not a sigh nor a tear, can abide while we trust and obey." Trust!

WEAKNESS WARNING: **Inferiority.** There is quite a difference between godly confidence and fleshly arrogance. Authenticity in us leaders validates that we realize we are nothing in and of ourselves; however, those we lead must never see an attitude or self-image of worthlessness in us. If we continually communicate this to those we lead, we will never get things right nor be able to complete the task God has given us, or we will fail because we are inferior to another; God's power in our lives becomes null and void. Please recall; God calls us to leadership. He equips and enables us to lead effectively for Him. Remember; He makes us into His Own personal leaders. We are not useless, hopeless, or worthless! Authenticity in us as leaders does not display inferiority, but it displays Christ-like confidence.

WEAKNESS WARNING: **Superiority.** On the other hand, arrogance and an attitude of complete superiority must not be found in an authentic leader. We must grasp the thought that others should not do what we say, just because **we** say it. Our leadership comes from the Word of God through the working of the Holy Spirit in our lives. If, as leaders, we must constantly remind those we lead to trust us, we deceive ourselves. An authentic leader needs not to demand trust and compliance from his followers. If we are pure in our leadership, people jump at the chance to follow us. Others see that God is working in the lives of us leaders, and they do not hesitate to get in on the action, and to be a valued part of it.

If we view ourselves as superior because we are leaders, we do not love others as Christ loves them. If we think we are superior because we are leaders, we think quite highly of ourselves and very little of those who follow us. A leader who believes that he is superior to others bases his acceptance of people upon many conditions.

If we fall into the trap of setting ourselves in a place of superiority, since we think God called us and not another, we devalue those we lead. When we devalue those precious saints who follow our leadership, we devalue their Creator and the gifts God has given them. At this point, we value ourselves as leaders higher than we value God. To remain completely authentic in his calling, a godly leader takes great care to guard against the attitude of superiority. We recognize that the more people we lead the more important God becomes; and the more insignificant we must become. In fact, the more authority we are given; the more servitude we are to display. The greater the number of people we lead, the greater our need is to seek God's guidance in leading them.

To avoid the oppression and bondage that comes from the leader of superiority, we must never desire loyalty, admiration, or validation from those we lead. If we hope for these things, we misguide our followers to focus on us leaders, therefore causing them not to focus on God. I think we believe, at times, that leading others requires tough love and strict boundaries. We consider those we lead with the idea that they cannot accomplish anything for themselves. Some may label it "hand-holding," some "coddling." We leaders sell ourselves on the idea that people **need** us to be superior to them, because people desire to be led.

If we leaders find a follower or two who will carry out our every wish upon beck and call, we offer them our good graces and, perhaps, a place of authority next to us. Authenticity in us leaders demands that our love for those we lead is unconditional and without self-exaltation. It is not our right to reward those who comply or restrain those who do not. On the contrary, God commands otherwise, admonishing us to regard others higher than we regard ourselves. God is the only Superior One!

If we approach our leadership role following the pattern of the humility of Jesus Christ, the will of God, and the guidance of the Holy Spirit, we will be authentic through and through. As leaders, we must admit our weaknesses and compensate for them. We must claim the power of God through the strengths with which He has gifted us. While we may appreciate our call to lead, since God has given it to us, we must focus diligently on following God's way and understanding; He put us here in the first place. We may claim the working of the Holy Spirit in our lives, but we must be adamant about allowing Him to be in control. Authentic leaders must guard every aspect of our leadership, so we do not become **frauds** for Christ.

Fraud Protection

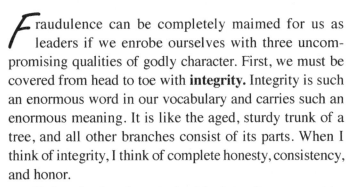

*F*raudulence can be completely maimed for us as leaders if we enrobe ourselves with three uncompromising qualities of godly character. First, we must be covered from head to toe with **integrity.** Integrity is such an enormous word in our vocabulary and carries such an enormous meaning. It is like the aged, sturdy trunk of a tree, and all other branches consist of its parts. When I think of integrity, I think of complete honesty, consistency, and honor.

To be a leader characterized by integrity, we must be completely honest. There is never an occasion or situation that requires us to lie, tell little white lies, and share half-truths as we lead others. If Jesus is our pattern for godly leadership, He **never** lied. Why should we?! While we as leaders are not perfect, we must be an example to the flock of God in giving our best effort to eliminate sin and emulate godliness in our lives. If we lead by example, we avoid lying at all costs. After all, it is listed as one of the Seven Deadly Sins. Imagine the horrific example we will be as leaders if we purposefully choose to commit one of the Seven Deadly Sins. Lies are always uncovered, and the liar is always exposed. God forgive me as a leader if I dare even to think of lying!

As godly leaders with integrity, we cannot separate lying from sharing half-truths. Half-truths are not complete truths. By disclosing part of something, we cause others to make assumptions, devise their own theories, or repeat portions of facts which lead to rumors. We have then become leaders who lead others to stumble, not to mention what we might do to the victim of the half-truth. In complete reality, we leaders may cause our followers to sin. If something is to remain in confidence, leaders must keep it in confidence. We have no authority to determine portions that may be exposed and portions that may not. Integrity requires that we leaders keep our tongues under control, never sharing half-truths.

To remain characterized by integrity in a world full of evil takes stamina, perseverance, determination, and drive as leaders who constantly think of those we lead. Our motives for leadership must be pure and selfless. Others must see this displayed in our actions each and every day. People must see us leaders remaining focused on what is godly, doing our utmost, never to turn from righteousness and truth. Our followers must see that we persevere, regardless of our feelings.

God's priceless sheep must be able to rely on leadership that remains consistent. A leader once said, "Vent up, not out." This is great advice, but I learned a hard lesson from that leader. To him, the advice was a mere proverb repeated diplomatically. The leader struggled to apply it in his personal life, so those who followed never applied it, either. Integrity is **who we are** and **what we do** as we lead. **Who we are determines what we do; what we do displays who we are!**

A leader of integrity remains consistent in all aspects of his life and leadership. Being committed to finish the things we start displays consistency; our personal Bible study, marriage covenant and parenting obligations, to name a few. Leading and loving others unconditionally in spite of our personal feelings displays consistency. Looking to God for direction and hope, regardless of our circumstances, proves consistency in our attitude towards adversity. Consistency proven in us leaders validates the quality of integrity within us.

To fully prove that we are leaders of complete integrity, a repetitive cycle should form from honesty, consistency, and honor. Pure honesty does not allow a lack of consistency. If it does, we appear inconsistent and untrustworthy, causing others to question our honesty as leaders. If we do not remain consistent in our leadership, those who follow us question our impartiality, fairness, and untainted judgment; therefore, we appear dishonest. If others view us as dishonest and inconsistent, they do not think of us as honorable leaders.

A leader of honor embodies honesty and truth, consistency and perseverance, and earns the respect and trust of those who follow him. A leader of integrity welcomes accountability in order to remain honorable, regardless of his positional leadership. Honesty, consistency, and honor bleed from the leader of integrity. The cycle repeats itself within our character, and God promises to bless us leaders because of our integrity.

The second uncompromising quality of godly, effective leaders is **sincerity**. Sincerity forms a barricade for us against fraudulence. Sincerity's evil nemesis and most formidable attacker is **hypocrisy**. Allow me to clarify what defines true hypocrisy and what does not.

A leader makes a decision, realizes that it was not the best decision, and then makes a second decision to replace the first. They are not a hypocrite. The leader simply changed his mind based upon the realization of what was not best. Let's say the leader of an evangelism program requires that all who follow in his ministry must complete thirty hours of evangelistic training, but the leader refuses to complete the training himself. That leader is, indeed, a hypocrite.

A parent who promises to purchase an expensive gift for his child and then cannot purchase the gift, since he finds himself unemployed, is not a hypocrite. The means for keeping the promise to the child no longer exists. On the other hand, say a parent promises an expensive gift to his child. The parent receives a substantial raise in wages but chooses to use the money to purchase something for himself. That parent is, indeed, a hypocrite.

A small group facilitator makes a long-term commitment to serve as host for the group's Bible studies. Demands of caring for an aging parent require that modifications be made to the facilitator's home. The time period for renovations and adjustments to take in the parent cannot be determined, and the facilitator can no longer keep his commitment to host or even fully participate in the small group ministry. This facilitator is not a hypocrite. Alternatively, a small group facilitator discovers that other activities are offered on the same nights as his Bible studies. In an attempt to participate in all activities, the facilitator withdraws the offer to host the Bible studies, due to other "commitments and demands." That small group facilitator is a hypocrite.

Sincerity is remaining committed to those we lead. It requires our sacrifice on behalf of our precious followers. A sincere leader determines to make every effort not to go back on his word or commitments. Sincerity makes no attempt to manipulate, control, or advance people and circumstances to work in our favor. Uncompromising sincerity in a leader prevents us from becoming bitter, angry, and divisive. Sincerity is never driven to deal harshly with others who may have a difference of opinion from ours. Like integrity, sincerity welcomes accountability and is never threatened by others who shine brighter than we leaders.

Some leaders mistake sincerity to mean "brutally honest." I once heard a leader say if he did not like you, he would not act like he did, because that would make him a hypocrite.

That same leader also stated he would never hold back on telling others "like it is." My heart is broken for this leader. As leaders, we must treat people, God's creation, with kindness regardless of how we feel about them. There is nothing hypocritical about that! God **does not like my sin** at all, but **He still likes me** and treats me with kindness. To adopt that leader's philosophy makes God a hypocrite! This heresy completely saddens me.

Likewise, speaking in a harsh manner, not holding back one's thoughts, and telling others "like it is" does not empower us as leaders. Some claim the cliché, "What you see is what you get!" then add, "Take it, or leave it. It's not my loss; it's yours." As leaders with pure sincerity, we must understand that God gives us great tools for assistance in dealing with others, whatever the case. He gives us wisdom and discernment when we ask. He gives us patience and grace on which to rely. Remarkably, He grants us godly discretion which enables us to lead people effectively without the need to be harsh, boldly untactful, and rudely forthright.

When sincerity is clearly evident in us, the leaders, those who follow welcome our thoughts, insight, and advice. Others respect what we have to say and who we are as leaders, since they **sincerely** perceive that we **sincerely** respect them and remain committed to their well-being in Christ. Purest sincerity is never brutal, aggressive, or motivated by hostility. Sincerity in the life of us leaders is tactful, full of strength, and motivated by complete love and respect for those we lead, no matter who they are or what they do.

The third full-proof quality with which a godly leader covers himself is that of **transparency**.

Leaders must have nothing to hide from those who follow us. Please understand. I mean in no way that we completely bare our souls before those who follow us. At times, when we attempt to share a personal experience for others to learn from it, it is easy to slip into self-absorption. We may plead with others. "Listen to me. Look what I did. I, I, I..." We neglect to share only what is absolutely necessary so all eyes and ears turn to God. Even unintentionally, we draw attention and emotional sympathy to ourselves as leaders before the listeners receive their unhindered opportunity to focus completely on God.

Sometimes, we simply talk too much! When we talk too much, most of what we say is meaningless, or it may become hurtful to others if we are sharing personal stories with all the participants named. We must be so careful that transparency does not morph us into blabbermouths or one seeking endless affirmation. **Transparency is revealed most in what we do, not in what we say.**

A leader who is completely transparent allows others to openly observe his character and work. If we lead with transparency, an attitude of defensiveness rarely exists within us. We do not find ourselves threatened by questions from others. Frustration and impatience subside when we must repeatedly encourage or guide those less mature in the faith. Sharing reasons or intentions for why we do what we do as leaders is commonplace in our leadership. We are not unnerved when others request explanations or information concerning the work within our leadership. Secrecy and ambiguity are never tactics that we use to approach those we lead.

In addition, "accountability" is not a forbidden word to the transparent leader. Like integrity and sincerity, transparency grasps onto godly, mature believers who can offer the accountability safety net to us as we lead. The safety lies in the fact that those who are able to hold us accountable ensure our best chances to remain honorable before God as leaders.

Accountability, however, is not defined as seeking advice from others. Seeking advice from wise council and accountability are two completely different things. Wise council is considered by the seeker, offers additional insight to the seeker, and provides a variety of godly perspectives for the seeker. A seeking leader may choose to accept or reject wise council, and the outcome of his choice is unlikely to be affected. Accountability offers success to us leaders in order to be holy, and it assists in binding the power of sin in our lives. It motivates us to be pure and do what is right, because we fear getting caught in doing what is wrong. The leader who refuses accountability, in a sense, has signed his own spiritual death sentence to sin. We have also sent the clear message that no one is capable of holding us accountable to godliness.

It is too easy to compromise our purity and cover our sin when we walk in leadership unobserved and unaccountable. Our acceptance of accountability as leaders proves to others that we desire to be transparent. We have nothing to hide, since all we desire is to serve God and lead others to serve Him in the greatest ways possible.

Transparency **does allow** our followers to see our weaknesses, foibles, and missteps as their leaders, but it also enables them to see God at work in our lives, just as He is in theirs. Think of the living picture this brings to those who follow due to the images they see clearly through us, their leaders. Oh, leader, this must be our heart's desire: complete, unhindered transparency.

Offering leadership with complete transparency can be pain-staking and terribly difficult for us as leaders. **Transparency requires sincere humility**. We know as leaders that we must be strong and decisive. Leadership demands that we take charge and accept the responsibilities that accompany leading. All the while, we must keep in mind that we are mere humans, susceptible to sin, and as fearful as others. We are equal in Christ to those we lead, but we are unequal to the level of accountability that comes with the responsibility of our leadership. We leaders must learn that the attitude of mutual equality in Christ brings us the respect and willful submission of those who follow us. We humbly earn their trust, not demand it!

Transparency automatically causes us to become vulnerable. Sadly, there are those who watch and wait, ready to pounce upon the leader that makes a mistake. Sometimes, ridicule comes from those we lead, as well as our peer leaders. The more we are transparent, the greater the amount of people who observe, draw conclusions about, and perhaps even criticize our aptitude as leaders. My perspective concerning transparency comes from an old sports adage, "No pain, no gain." The blessings and rewards of transparent leadership far exceed any pain or pressure we must endure because of it. The cost of transparency is great, but we cannot afford to lead without it! It is our protection against fraudulence and our insurance for authenticity.

The Glass House

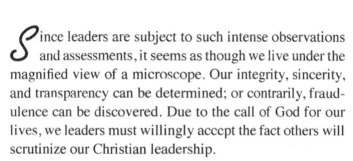

$\mathcal{S}$ince leaders are subject to such intense observations and assessments, it seems as though we live under the magnified view of a microscope. Our integrity, sincerity, and transparency can be determined; or contrarily, fraudulence can be discovered. Due to the call of God for our lives, we leaders must willingly accept the fact others will scrutinize our Christian leadership.

I am sure you have heard it said that pastors and their families live in glass houses. Every leader has grounds to make this claim. If we are passionate about and dedicated to leading with integrity, sincerity, and transparency, we are watched constantly. Whether it is we the leaders or others in our home, we are all observed and assessed upon the criteria that describe an effective or ineffective leader. A see-through house of glass perpetually surrounds us, and unrealistic expectations exist.

Anyone who passes by a leader's glass house has established his own personal perception, opinion, and vision of what they intend to see inside of it. It seems as though the spouse of a leader is to always be in agreement. Conflict is not permissible in the marriage relationship of leaders. Outsiders peering through the walls of the glass house believe that the couple inside still lives in a honeymoon stage of marriage. Terms of endearment must drip from the lips of one spouse to another. The toothpaste tube is squeezed correctly; the toilet seat is as it should be, and delectable dinners are on the table every night. The leader and his spouse must love one another endlessly. We must never disagree, and we must treat one another as if we were kings or queens. We wonder: Whose marriage is this?

When it comes to parenting, leaders are watched meticulously. It is completely out of the question that we ever have a need to scold our children, let alone discipline them. After all, the children of the leader, in spite of their own personalities and strong wills, are absolute angels! Our children must obey instantaneously, say "Sir" and "Ma'am," be neat and tidy, always share, and never fail at anything they try. The maturity level of our children must go far beyond that of most adults. Our young ones must make wise decisions continuously. We wonder: Whose children are these?

Looking through the walls, windows, and doors into the glass house, any spectator can see the true heart of us leaders. There is never a day that we leaders are tired or discouraged. There is no pain or tears in our house, only smiles and joy. Bible reading and prayer must take place twenty four–seven. If the lookers look long enough, they hope to actually see heavenly beings living among our family! We must be holy and consistent, so nothing terrible happens within our home. We must never lose our tempers, say words we regret, nor criticize others. We leaders do not face opposition or ill-intent. Answers to questions and biblical advice flow from our mouths in easy conversation.

Satan, he dares never to show up here! We wonder: Does Superman or Wonder Woman live here?

Obviously, the glass house is fictitious in existence but a figurative reality in the life of a leader. The perfect home, perfect family, and perfect leader are unreasonable and unattainable; yet for some reason, many people expect perfection from their leaders. As leaders, we often think we can never truly be genuine, because someone is **always** watching. There is no privacy in our home, not only from within, but also from without. There is no place in which to hide. We are vulnerable here. Whether we feel sad, happy, encouraged, uncertain, or confident, it can be viewed at any time within the glass house.

Our personal priorities are also clearly seen. Our strengths and weakness can become obvious through its walls. Our relationships and family dynamics are open to public view. Our friends and family members can see into our house; but notice, so can our enemies. Strangers may find our home very hospitable or very hostile. The faith of us leaders may clearly be seen, or anger and resentment might be in full view. Godliness may warm our home, or unrighteousness might make it dismal.

Those who follow a leader have frequent opportunities to look inside his glass house. Others have many opportunities to observe, evaluate, and determine an opinion of their leaders based on the display within the home. There is no gender, age, status, or life-season bias for those who are able to look inside. Leaders serve the complete Body of Christ, even if we are designated by our calling to focus on a specific group within it. The simple fact that we lead gives anyone a chance to see inside our glass house.

Our leadership peers also have opportunities to look inside the glass houses of one another. Among leadership, it is a challenge not to make unfounded comparisons or judgments. As colleagues in leadership and brothers and sisters in Christ, we must be first to edify and encourage our peers in leadership. Who can better relate to the struggles and disappointments of a leader than another leader? Who can understand the blessings and guidance of the Lord working in remarkable ways better than one leader to another? Who is better equipped to help carry the burdens and demands of leadership than one leader for another? Who is better able to offer accountability for a leader than one of his peers?

Quite honestly, for us leaders to see inside the glass houses of our brothers and sisters in Christ is a privilege and an honor for us. If we humbly keep our perspective as God's chosen leaders, we quickly realize that many of our peers far surpass us as effective, godly leaders. The view into their glass houses offers us motivation and inspiration to become better today than yesterday, and better tomorrow than today, in *our* leadership.

Foundation Blocks

Because my husband and I are both leaders called by God, our family has lived inside the glass house for many, many years. Has it been a challenge? Absolutely! Has it been unsettling? Certainly! Has it been revealing? Painfully! Did I ever regret it? Occasionally! Has it been worth it? I was unable to answer this question honestly until God recently showed me the purpose for our glass house. First, I noticed the foundations upon which God has been building over all these years.

Life's experiences and God's lessons have come year after year in our ministry. Those experiences and lessons have offered quite an unpredictable ride on the most erratic roller coaster ever. As my husband and I could never leave our assigned seats on this runaway train of sorts, I did not realize until just a short time ago God's meaning of the glass house and His reason for our dwelling within it. Through studying the Word of God, prayer, fasting, conversations with my husband, and memories of ministries past, God revealed to me His clear architectural plan for our glass house. As a leader called of God, I pray that my experiences and insight may offer you help and hope as you are a leader called of God. Together, we will come to understand the meaning of and reason for our glass houses.

To begin, after graduation, marriage, and our first baby, we jumped straight into full-time youth ministry. At that time, it was not uncommon for ministers to *wear many hats* within a church. Neil accepted a position as youth pastor, choir director (even though he could not read music), and congregational music leader (even though all he could do was sing and not direct). I was thrilled to be part of this congregation as a pastor's wife and brand new mother. Our first ministry! It was a Christian fairy tale in reality; however, it was only **my** reality!

Sadly, there are times in our lives when we are truly effective for the cause of Christ, and others feel threatened. Members of our new congregation, youth, and their families grew to love us. As people began to trust the integrity of our ministry, they were willing to accept changes and new ideas. Our philosophy of ministry has always been that of building relationships with those you serve, as well as implementing discipleship for them. People responded well to our methods. Things seemed to be moving forward so smoothly, until that one fateful day.

The majority of the congregation endeared us, but one seemed to despise us. The criticism came. A crotchety, wealthy, older woman approached the senior pastor of our church. She instructed him to speak to "that youth pastor" about his wife. "That girl wears her hair different every Sunday! If we hope to speak to her, we can never find her because she never looks the same!" It became her mission to find fault in our ministry any way she could, enlisting others to assist her. She was quite affluent, often blessing the church with tremendous financial gifts. We appreciated her ability to help the church in that way, but we never regarded her higher than those who could not. She did not appreciate our impartiality very much.

As a leadership example for this woman, my desire was to **put her in her place.** As leaders, we may need to consider confronting someone in love. Upon the wise council of my husband, who knew I was not really full of love at the time, I felt that I should be a leader who displayed graciousness instead of confrontation. Something as trite as my hairstyle was an issue for the woman. It did not have to be an issue for me, too.

As challenging as it was, I approached the woman every Sunday to personally say hello. After a short time, I could feel no anger or resentment towards her. In turn, she looked to see me every week and inquire as to how our baby boy was growing. As a leader, I finally realized that she wanted to be important to me, not because of her money, but because she wanted to care about me. She had no family members close to her, so she had hoped to care for us. While minimal damage and hurt had already occurred because others adopted her issue, it was easy to put it behind me and understand this older lady. At this time, God taught me my **first foundational leadership lesson: Help one feel good about one's self**. So it was our journey into the unknown territory of leadership began. We had taken our first steps.

God blessed our ministry work for some time in the church with the hairstyle debacle, but He did eventually move us to another place in which to lead. Once again, it was necessary to wear several hats of leadership. We attempted to lead teenagers, teach in a Christian school, coach basketball and cheerleading, coordinate the nursery ministry, lead the music ministry, mentor young couples, and coordinate holiday celebrations for the entire church family. When trying to be the leaders God wants us to be, it does pose a challenge at times to focus on more than one target group or task in leading.

Our tasks grew in number as we noticed the pastor's tasks rescinding. Completely baffled, we did not understand why leadership seemed to be removing itself. Church services became times of sharing testimonies or singing hymns. No message was given from the Word of God. Money began to disappear. My husband was told on a few occasions that he would not receive his contractual salary. We were deeply concerned because our son was a toddler at the time. I remember that our meals consisted of Cream of Wheat for breakfast, lunch, and dinner, lasting for over two weeks. It was soon after exposed that my husband's salary had been stolen by church leadership! Ironically, this was my **second foundational leadership lesson from the Lord: Know my limits!** This church has long been dissolved, but it is of utmost importance that we as leaders realize our physical, moral, ethical, and spiritual limitations as we lead.

Occasionally, God not only changed the ministries to which He took us, He also changed our geographical location. Moving, in and of itself, is always challenging. As we lead effectively in certain locations, we develop relationships and a comfort level in where we are. The attitude of feeling at home offers us security and stability. It allows us the opportunity to build friendships and relationships in Christ that are of tremendous value. Even we leaders do not care to be removed from the people we love and admire; however, God plants us where He wants us to grow and to grow others. In God's call to lead, He gives us the ability to accomplish what is difficult, like relocation. In this, my **third foundational leadership lesson** was revealed: **God moves with me**.

In continuing to reveal His foundations, God led us to somewhat of a large church for us to focus on ministering to youth and their families. At the time, the church was without a pastor to lead in this ministry. Lay-workers were very diligent and supportive as the church searched for a youth pastor. Pastoral leadership had requested that we step in to lead, even voluntarily for a season, until an official forum could be held to induct my husband into the staff position.

We served as youth ministry leadership for a little more than a year until the annual forum was conducted. As we served and awaited the forum, a long-time youth lay-leader began to resent losing any part of his leadership role. The leader began to compile a list of items that he did not care for regarding our leadership. In following, this leader requested a meeting to be held with additional pastoral staff, my husband, and me. As we sat in the office of the associate pastor, the youth leader placed a literal written list on his lap in sight of all of us. The list contained eighteen different criticisms and recommendations for my husband and me to address before the youth leader would support us in ministry leadership. Items on the list were unbelievably insignificant, without validation, and unnecessary. I am sure you now wonder about these critiques.

To appease your curiosity, one item listed was: Neil and Kim do not give the teenagers candy bars on their birthdays. Yes! This is absolutely true! At times, the associate pastor refrained from smirking and the slightest chuckle due to the ridiculousness of the items on the list. This pastor conducted himself with patience and discretion as an effective leader. My **fourth foundational lesson of leadership** was learned: **Distinguish personal preferences from biblical convictions**.

We realized that day that, even if we adapted to all the items on the list from the youth leader, another list would soon follow. As leaders, we cannot be easily offended when someone approaches us with a "list." We must understand the circumstances or motivation behind the person compiling it. With the support of the associate pastor, we respectfully revealed to the youth worker that we could not agree nor consent to all they had listed. We definitely cannot believe we lead so we will be pleasing to others and well-liked. We must learn to handle confrontation with wisdom and understanding.

In closing this chapter in our lives, the church held the annual forum. Strangely, my husband and I were not permitted to be a part of the meeting. It was discovered that the youth worker had been leading a long-time prayer group, specifically praying that we would never minister in their church. Unkind thoughts and criticisms were shared among a large group of people, some of whom had not yet met us. The lay-leader had caused so much division within the church, conclusive action could not be taken to affirm my husband as youth pastor for this ministry. While we were heart-broken and disappointed beyond words by the ordeal, we continued to lead and serve in that church for about another year. God blessed our ministry and gave us peace within the great turmoil, because we were able to continue leading in spite of others. Still in this church, I learned a **fifth foundational leadership lesson: Follow**

God's way, not man's way. As leaders, we must diligently learn to tell the difference between the two.

Another very significant foundation from the Lord was revealed to me during our time as senior pastor and wife. Initially, we went to the church for a different capacity, but there was a movement pending before we had arrived by which the church would be split. God took us to this church so when the split occurred, we would be there. In spite of this body of believers being torn apart, some from their closest family and friends, we had no intention of jumping ship. It was so sad to witness such a distraught congregation and hurtful experience. We knew we were sent there to lead and offer everything possible for an effective healing process to occur.

In beginning that healing process, it was necessary to select new members to the church leadership board and new leaders for program ministries. As shepherd and shepherdess, the responsibility fell upon us to pray, discern, seek wisdom, and equip new leadership to lead alongside us. Of course, God is so faithful. Newly chosen leaders within the church found themselves accomplishing things they never thought possible. Many came out of their comfort zones, attempting new things in which they found themselves successful. God was healing. He approved. **Foundational leadership lesson number six** was very obvious to me in this ministry: **Sometimes, I am just the ointment**. Leaders, we must recognize that we are used by God in the most unexpected ways and for the most undetermined times.

After several years, this church was restored, experienced growth, and continued to focus on the tasks of the ministry. Success came. As pastor and wife, we could not let our guard down one instant. Satan brutally attacks the leadership that is effective for Christ. Lackadaisical leaders accomplish nothing, so Satan has no need to worry about them. **Foundational leadership lesson number seven: Don't get lazy!** When things go well, we feel like we can sit back and relax. We think too highly of what we have accomplished. Leaders need to understand that, while we rest in God, we must continue to strive against sin, complacency, and mediocrity.

After quite some time and complete restoration to the ailing church, God called us away to restore and rebuild a ministry for youth and their families in a different church. There was no question in our minds that God called us to the new church, a new flock of sheep, and a place that would occupy a special corner in our ministry hearts. God's affirmation of more foundations was certain.

The transition from the old ministry to the new was smooth and completely led by God. The peace of our hearts and minds was indescribable as we watched God lay out the clear plan of His will for our lives. I was able to teach, and my husband could focus on ministering to youth and their families. The power of God was completely relevant to us; we could not deny that God was using and blessing us. It was humbling, amazing, overwhelming, invigorating, and even somewhat unnerving to see such work from our Lord and Savior, Jesus Christ! Oh, we were a part of it every day — how tremendous! As leaders, we constantly fought against personal pride.

As we faithfully continued to lead the young people, we witnessed wonderful spiritual growth within them. We saw some come to accept Jesus Christ into their lives. We developed relationships, not only with the young people, but also with their families. At times, there were missteps. What leader never stumbles? We knew this was God's ministry, and He was working in and blessing it. Dear leader, be joyful and thank God as you see Him working. Tell Him, "Thank you for using me!"

Over time, we noticed small challenges cropping up against us and God's work. A student or two was never satisfied with our focus, the teaching, or the impartiality of our leadership. One parent often requested meetings, stressing that my husband not disclose the meetings to the parent's spouse or children. Despite much effort and energy to reach out to these people, nothing ever satisfied them. Satan was throwing his first round of darts at us!

After many years in ministry leadership, we recognize that we will never please everyone all of the time. We cannot predict ill motives. In times like this, God exposes the intent of Satan to use even wonderful people as a distraction to hinder the work of God from being accomplished. As leaders with the lives of so many others at risk, we understood we could not remain focused on such distractions from Satan. We had to remain focused on the direction of God.

As time continued to pass, we began noticing unusual occurrences within the church. Attendance began to decline consistently. Sermons were often delivered with a tone of anger and judgment. The messages were, sometimes, communicated with biblical inaccuracy or loaded with personal vengeance. Some leaders received excessive amounts of flattery, affirmation, and gifts, while other leaders were ostracized and cut off. Church members having concerns and questions were ignored, criticized, and instructed to keep quiet. Meetings requested by members of the congregation with church leaders were denied, or they were forced to meet in secrecy with a designated leader. God's sheep seemed to have no voice. Satan's barricades became stronger.

Leadership staff meetings were cancelled, but some leaders still met in secret. My husband was excluded from meetings, and this caused great concern for us regarding the unity of the church leadership. As leaders, we must remember to be aware of those we lead, but we must also be aware of those who lead alongside us. **Foundational leadership lesson number eight** became quite clear: **We are a team**. Regardless of the size of the ministries or organizations that we lead, it takes more than **just one** to lead the Body of Christ. It is our responsibility to affirm and accept the capabilities of others who lead along with us. Jesus did not choose one disciple. He hand-selected twelve and then told them to make more disciples.

The intentional separation of my husband from others in leadership became clear soon enough. We personally witnessed things in the church that caused great concern within our spirits. These things displayed the workings and unclear motives of church leaders. Integrity appeared questionable. Programs were altered. Leaders in various ministries resigned or were removed from their leadership roles. The turnover and inability to maintain consistent, godly leadership became upsetting. Secrecy and lying were normal leadership practice. Under immeasurable conviction from the Holy Spirit, my husband shared his concerns with leadership. These concerns were so overwhelming to bear, while handling the personal challenges we were facing simultaneously.

At the same time, we experienced massive changes and great sorrow in our family. Since the youth ministry was truly being blessed of God, Satan loaded all cannons to war against us, relentlessly. We began feeling discouraged and beaten up, if you will, after so many years of battle in leadership. My husband and I began to question whether we were in the right place, at the right time, doing the right things for God. In confidence, my husband shared our struggles with another leader, requesting prayer and insight.

While earnestly praying to the Lord for confirmation our youngest, our daughter, went off to college. Leaders experience empty nest just like anyone else. We were so sad, and yet so joyful to see her go. We were deeply saddened because our daughter is such an amazing young lady. She grew up too quickly, and we did not want her to leave. We remain joyful as we constantly think of what God has done, is doing, and will do in her life. She attends a Christian college, maintains academic excellence while playing on the women's soccer team, works as a staff assistant, and is growing in her walk with God. She is quite the leader for such a young woman!

In addition our oldest, our son, relocated from next door to purchasing his home in the next town. This is not a huge distance; but instead of spontaneous, almost daily visits with our son and granddaughter, we must now plan times of visitation. This is not a big deal; but if you are a parent or grandparent, you can understand my feelings. While our son remains our child, he is also a great person of strength and support to us. He has accomplished his college degree, is successful in his career field, and is a devoted dad, overcoming some tough opposition and persevering through some hard-knock life lessons. We admire his strength and perseverance tremendously.

Likewise, we share many priceless moments with our granddaughter, such as: cooking, baking, making crafts, gardening, and playing games. She is our pride and joy! My husband and I will never forget the night she crawled up beside me on the couch and told us that she asked Jesus into her life that day. We have numerous conversations about God and the wonderful things He does in our lives. Who, in their right frame of mind, would want those times to be limited?!

While continuing through our time of prayer and discouragement, my father-in-law died. His story is so simple, yet remarkable. He received Jesus into his life and was baptized at the age of eighty. My mother-in-law and he attended the church where my husband led as senior pastor. My husband had the joy and privilege of leading my father-in-law to Christ and baptizing him. Our family felt great sorrow when he passed, but we greatly rejoiced because he is with Jesus. My husband and his older brother, who is also a pastor, conducted the funeral service. You would have thought we attended a party!

In conclusion, while we continued to lead in youth ministry, we questioned our calling to continue. My husband shared deep, heartfelt concerns in confidence with leadership. Our hearts were heavy as church leadership appeared to lose sight of God, not maintaining integrity. Our daughter left home. Our son and granddaughter moved away. Our parent died. Satan beat us to the ground. We asked ourselves if things could become worse.

One evening, in a definitive moment, God completely confirmed through a sincere working of the Holy Spirit in the hearts of our teenagers that we were indeed in the right place, for the right thing, at the right time. God definitely called us to lead in this church. We were certain.

Sadly, however, things did get worse just a short time later. Leadership requested a meeting with my husband. The pastor and two others told my husband he was removed from his position in the church. No reasons or performance criticisms were documented, validated, or spoken. There were none. This fell on us like a hard, lead balloon, because we are veterans in leadership. We led in complete truth and honesty at this church. The hastiness and harshness used to eliminate us was completely devastating and confusing. That day, God showed me His **ninth and final foundational leadership lesson: Integrity, sincerity, and transparency can cost you everything**!

Full Disclosure

Keep in mind, through all of the experiences and lessons in leadership, we continued living in our glass house. God's foundational lesson blocks were revealed and able to be seen by others. To this day, thousands of people have had the opportunity to peek inside our house, unannounced. What have all those people seen within our glass house over the years? With uninhibited honesty and complete disclosure, this is what I believe spectators have seen.

In the days of "the Hair Debacle," those peering inside our glass house would have seen our young pastor's family. They would have seen my wise, charismatic young husband who remained even-tempered and patient as he advised me on how to handle a crotchety, older church member. I would have been seen wondering: Why is this lady picking on me? Over time, our young leaders' hearts softened as we came to understand the motivation behind the lady's criticisms.

As we continued dwelling in the glass house when wearing far too many ministry hats, people looking inside would have viewed a very weary youth pastor and his wife. Confusion and disappointment would have been seen on our faces, since we were still immature in our leadership roles. We had not yet learned how to stay continually focused on God in spite of the circumstances that surrounded us. Many tears fell in anger; a leader had hurt our family. Frustration bounced from one spouse to the other, because someone had to take the blame for our awful situation. Fear and discouragement were battled daily, for we were faced with finding some type of monetary provision. Eventually, frowns of bitterness and anger turned to smiles as we saw God provide in miraculous ways. The table was again set for dinner, without Cream of Wheat!

One thing about living in the glass house is that no matter where you go, it goes with you! This is a very unique and incomparable feature about this house. In God relocating our glass house, He has granted more opportunities to more visitors in which to observe. In such cases, those peering through the glass would have seen our family up to our noses in boxes and plastic totes. Every carton would have been labeled, and a box was set aside with cleaning supplies with which to sanitize after the move. Viewers would have seen that our family was completely exhausted and a bit apprehensive about learning the topography of a new city or state; however, we adapted well to moving, because we did it together. God gave us a new, exciting place in which to lead.

Living in the glass house during the years of "the Eighteen List," our family discovered things about leadership that had not yet been discovered. We would have been viewed as committed and dedicated to serving the Lord. On-lookers would have seen us trying very hard to meet the expectations of those who followed us. Creative ideas came regularly, causing us to form effective leadership. We would have been caught questioning the motives of others and wondering why we posed a threat to other leaders.

Many guests entered our house, so many had a direct line of sight from all dimensions. There were no secrets there. Over time, dings and cracks would have been seen in the house's glass.

Hurt, confusion, and devastation had caused our family to attempt covering up our glass house. Could anyone be stopped from peering inside? We considered abandoning our home.

With the passing of time, we worked hard and repaired our glass house's dings and cracks. Restoration took place on the inside, as well as on the outside. With our house in like-new condition, our family continued to follow God's call for us to lead in "the Broken Church." Others scoping out our house would have seen us leaders seeking the healing power of God. We knew we could not cover the wounds of our new church with a figurative bandage, but somehow we had to embody the healing ointment that it needed. Anyone passing by our glass house would have witnessed our strong faith and perseverance. Prayers would have been whispered daily, so we could continue to embody the healing ointment and not a fly in it. Spectators would have witnessed our passionate leadership full of integrity, sincerity, and transparency. While we worked to heal others, hard times of personal refinement also came to us. In plain sight of all, we would have to sustain ourselves in the strength of the Lord to make it through the refiner's fire.

Continually, God has secured and protected our glass house and our family within its walls. The toughest storm that our home has had to withstand was that of "the Most

Expensive Ministry." Oh, what a challenge it was holding up one if its walls, while stretching to keep another from crashing down! Passers-by would have seen our family at peace and in chaos all at the same time. They would have been able to hear the cries of devastation and disappointment, yet they also heard rebukes against evil.

On one day, people viewing inside would have seen our courage, determination, and fortitude to continue in leadership for God, regardless of our circumstances. On another day, those looking inside would have seen confusion, uncertainty, and a where-do-we-go-from-here expression on our faces. Viewers would have seen us searching Scripture for answers and guidance. They would have noticed that we were baffled and blind-sided. Many saw the injustice and wrong against us, yet very few would speak against it. With great effort, prayers were constantly whispered, for we were faced with an abrupt, unfounded removal from leadership after so many dedicated years. The question would have been asked: Will our house make it through this particular storm?

Home Repairs

*T*he saying goes: You never know what you're really made of until what you're made of is challenged or exposed. These challenges, whether attacks from Satan or tests from God, can either discourage or refine a leader and his family. We know that when God is working mightily through us and within us, Satan **will** work mightily against us. Herein lies the challenge: The extreme exposure of who and what we really are! With us leaders living in glass houses, **everything** will be exposed to **everyone**.

Following our costly, enormous storm, it was necessary to begin repairing our house right away. One of the greatest lessons leaders must learn throughout life is to enlist help when needed. There is no way we leaders can know and accomplish everything life has with which to test us. In our world today, there are so many people who are trained and educated to perform numerous tasks that extend far beyond their ability. While leading, an effective leader is smart to surround himself with such valuable people. In developing a plan to repair our glass house, we "contracted" specialists in their own rights.

Throughout our lives, we have been blessed with a group of very special friends and co-leaders with whom we served. Some have been in our lives as far back as the days of my husband's teenage years. Others have come into our lives in recent years. Nonetheless, these devoted Christians were ready and well-armed to provide us with the disaster relief of prayer and encouragement after what was labeled our most deadly storm.

To begin, the needs of our repairs were prioritized. After such a blow, it was necessary to restore and strengthen our hearts and minds before working on the external surroundings of our God-given glass house. We knit together as a group and joined with saints across the globe for a forty-day time of prayer, Bible study, and fasting. We searched the Scriptures and prayed, so God could show us His plan concerning the situation. It was remarkable and overwhelming to see our day-to-day Scripture readings unfold before us! God's wisdom came with miraculous guidance. He definitely provided for and sustained us while facing such a great unknown and deep hurt.

A question that haunted me deeply upon my husband's removal was: How does one leader have complete authority with which to remove another leader from ministry? While there is a proper order of professional submission for leadership within churches and organizations, I was unable to grasp the ability of one individual to place himself above all others in ministry leadership. This torment had to be resolved in order for me to move forward with my in-home repairs. After all, my biblical perspective of ministry leadership, in the church particularly, is that all pastors are equal in the call of God. Each may focus on specific groups of people, but all have equal calling. After the forty days of prayer, searching God's Word, fasting, and deliberation with wise counselors, God gave me unobstructed vision to see the answer quite clearly.

In the church, staff order may be senior pastor, associate pastors, elders, or church board members. All those named are leadership. All **are equal** in receiving a direct call from God to lead. All **are equal** in the Body of Christ. All **are equal** as sinners who have been redeemed. All **are equal** in having to give an account for those we lead. All **are equal** in the expectations to live as examples for others. All **are equal** in the eyes of God, for we will each answer to Him at the final time of judgment for our own doings. All **are equal** in the expectations for us to know and teach the Scriptures. The senior pastor is the only leader who will additionally be held accountable for their leadership of all, and including all other leaders. **How can one leader completely remove another leader from ministry?** Biblically, he cannot.

Healing continued as I understood my own personal, God-given authority as a leader. A friend said, "Your husband has been wrongfully removed from a position, but he has **not** been removed from leadership." No one except God can remove us from leadership ministry. This falls contingent upon the fact that we leaders have never led immorally, unethically, or illegally. In such a case, we remove ourselves from leadership; and unless true repentance is offered, we are completely unworthy to claim any calling from God to lead others.

In the solution, I also understood that God allowed the will of man to prevail, so His ultimate will could be accomplished. Through the wisdom from Scripture, it became clear to us that the church leadership was turning its heart from God and toward pleasing themselves. God's permitted removal of us from the church by way of our terrible storm was His protection for our philosophy of leadership: **integrity, sincerity, and transparency**. You see, God no longer wanted us to remain in **a neighborhood** that was not pleasing to Him. God allowed us to be removed and then provided a great opportunity for my husband to lead in a different place, in a different way, while meeting our daily needs. Inside home repairs have been accomplished!

We must recognize that home repairs take place in stages. At times, we find that as we begin to repair structural damages, something else has been exposed that we did not yet notice. Because of the process and steps taken to accomplish one type of repair, it uncovers other areas of weakness, vulnerability, or wear-and-tear. When we are in the process of glass home repairs as leaders, it is to our greatest advantage to address any discoveries immediately. If we feel we can brush issues aside, neglect them, or completely attempt to cover over them, it will be detrimental to all who live inside, visit, or view our home. While repairs are often time-consuming, costly, and very inconvenient, they are never unaffordable to us who are passionate about leading in truth and righteousness.

Most often, an area of our home needs repairing only once. After that, it is as good as new! The old proverb states: An ounce of prevention is worth a pound of cure. The cost for the ounce is, out-right, far less than the forthcoming pound. God's chosen leader, it is our greatest advantage to have courage, admit our areas of inadequacy and flaws, and then jump at the chance to fix them. It benefits us tremendously to repair one issue, thoroughly, in its

proper time, as opposed to facing the completely dilapidated, condemned home of the future. Please, do it! Our
God-given glass house will remain standing firm on its
blessed foundations if we do.

Fixer-upper

*T*hroughout a long tenure of leadership, especially within the same ministry group or organization, it might be that we have become unfeeling or stagnant in leading. We have "been there, done that, and seen it all." Sometimes, we leaders make compromises to continue leading where we should not, because no one else is able to step up. Sometimes, we think others do not respect our leadership, so we adopt the attitude, "Why fight it?" Sometimes, we are so set in our own ways as leaders that no one else dares challenge us or offer new ideas. Perhaps, we think, no one can or will lead better than we do ourselves.

Regardless of the reason, our glass houses have become dilapidated and untouched, since we do not see the need to improve anything within ourselves. Those who follow our leadership see our house as uninviting, condemnable for habitation, and in a neighborhood on the wrong side of the tracks. We argue with others, are strong-willed, and are determined to be the highest of the high. We might even go so far as to say: If you think poorly of my house, you do not have to look at or visit it. Please leader, stop and look intently! Indeed, we may be in need of massive renovations.

To once again become effective as leaders who please the Lord and lead others successfully, we must do the **very** hard work. A fixer-upper home displays a house that has been in a poor state for an extended period of time. It means problems were deeply hidden and avoided for years. As strong, effective leaders, we must **honestly and thoroughly** inspect every corner of our hearts. There may be the desecration of pride, resentment, bitterness, sin against others, or hidden sin buried within the dilapidation. We may use excuses such as blaming things on our difficult pasts, our lack of education, or ignorance to keep us from admitting that our glass house needs a great deal of work. Rejection of the Holy Spirit's control in our leadership and determination to maintain our control hinders the potential for the beauty of our home to be seen.

The fixer-upper process is not enjoyable, is not pleasant, and can leave no stone unturned. Sometimes, walls are completely demolished, rooms gutted, and the sledge hammer hit brutally hard. It is lengthy, intimate, humiliating, and unsettling. It requires us leaders to be submissive, humble followers as we feel indescribable pain. It means confessing sin and requesting forgiveness from God and others. It demands the improving of ourselves.

Reconciliation to God and with others is the process to firmly restore the foundation on which we must again attempt to build. We must return to the roots and proper foundations of our calling. If we are godly leaders, we yield to receiving support and accountability from other mature Christians so complete restoration may take place. While it challenges us, we must admit the mistakes we have made, recognize any wrong ways in which we have led our followers, and follow every step of God's blueprint in Scripture to rebuild unity with God and others. This is difficult for us leaders, because it means forgetting and forsaking grudges or hurt. Yes! This process is extremely pain-staking. Yes! It is absolutely necessary if we do not want to find our glass house in complete rubble. In earnest, dear leader, we must fix up!

This process continues slowly, but consistently. It may take us just a few days or weeks, or it could take a few years. It may require a complete heart and life make-over in us, the leaders, or it might require a ripple effect of repentance, restoration, reconciliation, and redirection that only begins with us, the leaders.

Fixing up our dilapidated home requires direct attention be given to very specific areas: the foundation, the inside, the outside, the attic, the basement, the yard, the walkways, and most importantly, our family inside. It means realizing that some of the features of our former glass house may never be included within the new one. It means finding a proper place in our new home for the things that are of value and worth saving from the old. It means some of the passageways in our old house must be completely sealed, never to be used again. It means that we as leaders understand that this process not only affects us; it also affects our family, friends, and followers.

In addition, we must admit that the processes to restore our fixer-upper may cause displacement. As the owner of a glass house, we might find ourselves temporarily removed from it. God is so good to protect us, even from ourselves. In order to purge the house and purify it for further progress, it may be too dangerous for us to remain in it while adjustments are being made. It is by the grace of God that He does not allow the house to fall on us. God facilitates our renovations.

Others may see that we have been temporarily evicted and massive reconstruction is occurring within our home. We may be completely humiliated and embarrassed. Once the work is done, we can return with honor to all things new! We can walk into and reside in our beautiful fix-er-upper. We will see that the dividends of such a sacrificial investment were well worth it. Thanks and praise to God that He is the Master Builder! He has re-established and restored our home to be admired by all who pass by it.

The Un-welcome Mat

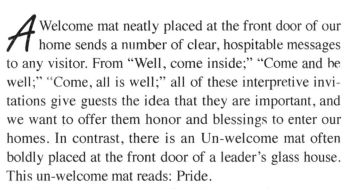

*A*Welcome mat neatly placed at the front door of our home sends a number of clear, hospitable messages to any visitor. From "Well, come inside;" "Come and be well;" "Come, all is well;" all of these interpretive invitations give guests the idea that they are important, and we want to offer them honor and blessings to enter our homes. In contrast, there is an Un-welcome mat often boldly placed at the front door of a leader's glass house. This un-welcome mat reads: Pride.

The un-welcome mat of Pride adamantly makes the statement to our visitors: "Pfuh-ride on by! You are not welcome here. You are not good enough to enter." At our doorstep, leaders must be very conscious of the message sent to those who pass by our glass home. Pride creeps into our hearts for many reasons, but we cannot make any excuses for it.

The un-welcome mat of Pride may appear because we have faced years of battle in our leadership. We no longer desire to be compassionate as we start to think, "They just had it coming!" Perhaps we have been blessed with great success as Christian leaders, and we fail to keep diligent watch for pride's deceptive arrival in our hearts. We see ourselves as absolutely amazing! Maybe we take the view that leadership is superiority, and no one has the right to see inside our home. We think, "They do not deserve it at all!"

Likewise, it is very easy for a leader to think, "My home is **my** one place of refuge. No one can judge me here." This perspective can lead to a struggle with self-pity. Self-pity leads to an attitude of keeping people at arm's length so they no longer hurt us. Keeping people at arm's length makes us unapproachable. Being unapproachable sends a message: I have no interest in you. Having no interest in others as a leader is solidly rooted in pride. Our un-welcome mat clearly states: I am not transparent as a leader, no matter what the reason behind it.

Please recall that transparency is not the complete, uninhibited, tactless baring of our souls. Our welcome mat does not say: "Come in and disrespect me as your leader." It does not imply that we will be the doormat of another to be trampled upon with the intent to harm and hate. It does not extend the invitation for everyone to enter upon their own discretion without considering our preference first. It does not communicate that we are receptive to lying, evil will, gossip, dissension, secrecy, and joining with others who hope for us to become partners in sin.

As leaders, we must focus on the kind, loving, and mature motivation behind placing the welcome mat at our door in the first place. We must also be care-takers on con-stant alert, so the un-welcome mat of Pride never finds a place on our doorstep. A leader once adopted a rather harsh quote from a well-known Hollywood star. The lengthy diatribe of the star stated all the things in life, they were determined **to refuse**. The Christian leader chose to adopt the quote of the star as his personal philosophy of life and leadership. This Christian leader affirmed how definite the quote "is me!" The quote listed the refusal "to love others who did not love me, to desire to please anyone but one-self, to accept others negativity, to waste time and energy on others or things that did not lift me up, and many more of the same."

Sadly, the leader placed the un-welcome mat of Pride (Pfuh-ride on by; you're not welcome here) at the front door of his God-given, unconditional, loving glass home. The entire mantra was laced with the right to reject others because they do not please me or assist in my life's agenda. The quote did not include helping others with their weak-nesses, loving even though I may not be loved in return, doing good things to and for others, not returning evil for evil, or taking the high road. My heart breaks for those hurting and confused who pass by this leader's glass house and read such an un-welcome mat. No one can predict how many will be rudely turned away.

For leaders, there may be times when we wish we could conceal our welcome mat. Because we are still emo-tional people, regardless of our calling, we may experi-ence a need to withdraw from public service and view. It is natural, particularly in times of refinement, distress, or weariness. With the honorable call of God to lead, we may never replace our Welcome mat with the Un-welcome mat.

If we must take a step back to regain our perspec-tive as leaders, it is most beneficial for those we lead to place the "Will return at...[time]" sign on the door; all the while leaving the Welcome mat in its proper place. If our followers have seen our welcome mat inviting them in, they recognize their leaders are people too, and we may need a little time for ourselves. Because we have earned their respect and willful submission, those who follow will respect our need for personal time with God or family. They understand they are still welcome, just not at **that** time.

Spring Cleaning

In our home, spring cleaning is one of my personal favorite times of the year. While I appreciate antiques, historic heirlooms, and primitive collectibles, it is always enjoyable for me to go "out with the old and in with the new." I am not at all a pack-rat. I thrive when things are organized, neat, and useful. To me, one can have too much stuff that is of absolutely no use. I have not kept every hair cut from my children's heads or lost baby teeth from their mouths. Many precious things move me, but I am not a sentimental symphony. It seems people often keep things just for the sake of keeping them. I do not!

Whether we leaders reside in a brand new glass house, an established one, or a fixer-upper, purging and purifying is essential to keeping our leadership consecrated before God and others. With the passing of time, it is easy for a leader to acquire quite a collection. Our collection may be one of leadership methods based upon the philosophy of, "This is how I've always done things." It may be a collection of the inclusion of the same people within our inner circle for use in our personal agendas. The collection may be a portfolio of "I's:" I have done this; I have accomplished that; I have developed the program; I have…, I have…, I have! It may be a collection of practices inherited from one who has led before us.

For whatever reason and to whatever extent, traits within our leadership style, methods, and desires easily collect and define us as leaders. They pile up in excess so subtly that they overtake every aspect of our personal, spiritual, and leadership lives. These collections occupy space in our hearts and minds and they completely eliminate any room for godly characteristics to dwell, let alone offer godly inspiration for our leadership.

Routinely, we as leaders must set aside times for extensive prayer, fasting, Scripture reading, and soul-searching. Just as spring cleaning in the home removes what is unnecessary, useless, and cluttering, a thorough cleaning of our heart and soul gives us the opportunity to remove all that is unnecessary, useless, and ungodly within us. A well cleaned-out leader in heart leads purely, shines brightly, and displays righteousness as the master of his glass house and care-taker of his flock. We beam with integrity, sincerity, and transparency!

Thorough spring cleaning digs deep into the nooks and crannies of the home. It searches in depth, into the dark corners of the closet, and under the heavy pieces of furniture that are rarely moved. Spring cleaning is effectively completed when the process travels from room to room in planned sequence. It requires tough scouring and scrubbing at times; for you see, dirt has built up over time. The dirt, grime, and abundant cobwebs must be removed. Oh, leaders, may we have the courage to roll up our sleeves, get down on our hands and knees (literally), and cleanse our hearts from the dirt residue that hinders our godly leadership. We must not neglect any nook or cranny, dark corner, or heavy issue in any area of our hearts. As others clearly see us in our glass houses, may we be truly pure like the glass itself. May the glass sparkle and shine with the glory of the Lord and the illumination of the Holy Spirit living inside, abiding in us. Spring cleaning, a necessary process, is vital for leaders.

Neighbors

*H*ave you ever heard the saying, "Beware of neighbors bearing gifts?" Within the figurative neighborhood of the leader's glass house, there reside neighbors of many kinds. Because we are an example to those who follow and witness our leadership, unexpected affirmation or gifts may be given. Gifts are most often a way of expressing the giver's love and admiration to the recipient of the gift. Occasionally, gifts might be given with ulterior motives and must be received by us leaders with caution and understanding. For leaders, we must not necessarily judge the heart of a gift-giver, but it is our responsibility to be aware of their motives.

A leader loved a certain food. This leader volunteered his passion for the food in any public setting. Following the leader's proclamations, gifts of the food appeared for many days on the desk of the leader. This poor, disillusioned leader received the gifts of food as a method of affirmation and admiration from those he led. Repetitive statements of the leader's fondness for the food incited responses from the followers to give, therefore making the leader feel good about his leadership. This leader did not recognize that he continually led the followers to seek honoring their leader and not the Lord. Whether this took place intentionally or unintentionally, we leaders must be so careful in understanding **why** gifts are given. As godly leaders, we must never incite gift-giving for our own, personal benefit.

As in the example of the leader and the food gifts, gifts come in different forms. There are many mature, generous, and kind people within the flock of God who sincerely hope to bless their leaders. They choose giving the leader a tangible gift to express appreciation. We desire appreciation as leaders. Leading is hard and, sometimes, a thankless calling, so a little appreciation goes a long way. It is the repetitive, bigger and better gift-giving with which we must be concerned. How might we as leaders graciously and respectfully handle this type of gift-giver?

We must be wise to determine the motivation behind the giving of a gift. Does the gift happen to come with the "you scratch my back, I'll scratch yours" persona attached? Does it come from a giver who he, himself needs to be affirmed by us, the leaders? Does it come from a need within one to outshine others in the eyes of his leader? Does the gift come from someone who is misguided about generosity and genuine motives for giving to others? As leaders, we can easily assist such a giver to continue to give, but with pure motives. We can imagine a scenario.

Perhaps we are given a gift card to a favorite restaurant. Because we want those who follow us to focus their eyes on God and not on us, we might express our sincere, heartfelt appreciation to the gift-giver. Following our gratitude, we may discretely ask if the giver realizes that another precious saint has been going without meals. We inquire if either we can share the meal with the person in need or pass the gift card along to them entirely.

Make no mistake, leader. We must never offend the giver of any gift; but if the practice is repetitive and meant to puff us up, we must tastefully redirect the intentions of the giver. We have no need, so we direct their eyes toward someone who does need. The blessings from God in this process are abundant. First, He blesses us, the leaders, for leading sacrificially and unselfishly. He blesses the gift-giver for meeting the need of another. God also uses this teachable moment for us leaders to show our followers to be generous, unselfish, and to become need-seekers. Lastly, God blesses the one who truly has the need with provision from Himself through the hands of a leader and another saint. In this process, God is honored and glorified. This is a win-win for everyone!

Some gifts come in the form of praise, affirmation, and verbal accolades. Dear leader, we must beware of endless songs of praise completely directed toward us. A gracious, "Thank you for kindness," coming from another is adequate. We do desire to hear that we have done a fantastic job, or that our hard work and efforts have been noticed. Leaders are no different than followers when it comes to our desire to receive commendations; but, we leaders may never be driven by words of man's praise, nor can we become affirmation junkies. We then are willing recipients of shallow flattery. We do not deserve recognition above others just because we are leaders. Remember, the more we are praised, the higher the standard to live up to. Isn't leadership already hard enough?!

Helping others praise our wonderful God instead of singing our praises can be accomplished quite simply. If we hear praise directed toward us, we offer gratitude to those people who have mustered the courage to say something positive and uplifting to us. Immediately, we praise and thank God along with others, and then direct them to thank God for what He has done through us. Request that the praise-giver offer thanks to God for several days for the good they have witnessed in us, their leaders. This results in consistent prayer and praises given to God on our behalf instead of mere words spoken to us that easily inflate and misguide our egos. We lead a follower in a pattern of prayer and praise to God as we take this approach to receiving praise and affirmation. The leader pleases God, the flock pleases God, and God is pleased!

There is a saying in our family for giving gifts at Christmas and birthdays. We say; "Just give money; it always fits, and you never have to return it!" Money gifts seem to make everyone who receives them quite happy. Leaders may be the recipient of money gifts at times. We must approach reception of such gifts with ethical caution. Personal gifts of money are indeed separate from charitable money gifts; but due to our position in public view, we leaders must maintain godly morals and ethics in receiving money from any generous giver. We must never allow one who follows us to bestow money gifts on us routinely. The motivation behind these money gifts might appear questionable, as well as the moral standards of the leader receiving them. Leaders must never appear as though we can be bought.

Money gifts given to a leader other than on special occasions or by sincere prodding from the Holy Spirit upon a giver can be tactfully managed. Again, it may be suggested to the money gift-giver that there is another who has tremendous needs. Request the approval to share or pass on the financial gift. The same lessons in handling the gift card can be applied here.

In addition, it may be necessary for us leaders to kindly and respectfully say, "Thank you, but no thank you." Encourage the giver to bless others beyond us leaders. Suggest they consider a missionary, sponsor a child to attend Christian summer camp, or purchase the poor widow's monthly prescription which she cannot afford. Options for pure financial gift-giving are endless and return immeasurable blessings from the Lord on their investments. We leaders are immeasurably blessed as we lead people to focus on God, others, and the work of the ministry, instead of the leading worker of the ministry.

Leaders must realize, because we live in our glass houses, the manner in which we receive gifts can be obvious. Over time, others may notice or become well aware of the who, what, when, and why in the gift-giving process. The worst case for us leaders is that the entire process becomes one that elevates us, misleads the giver, and indirectly belittles others who are not capable nor desire to offer gifts to us.

Again, keep in mind that gift-giving is a tangible way in which many communicate their love for another in our culture. Whether gifts are very small or extremely large, they are most often used to communicate affection. There is nothing wrong or impure in communicating appropriate love and affection to another. In receiving such gifts, sincere gratitude and appreciation for the sacrifice on the part of the giver is mandated. It is not within our authority as leaders to deny a follower of their potential blessings from God as they give to Him, others, or us with a pure heart.

It is the leader's responsibility to discern, consider, and understand the motivation behind gift-giving. We must beware of neighbors bearing gifts, over and over and over again.

Neighborhood Watch

*W*hen I think of neighborhood watch programs, my mind recalls the images I have seen portrayed on television shows. The busy-body, nosey neighbors keep constant watch on all the homes in their neighborhood. They notice every detail about every resident, their families, and their lifestyles. With uninhibited passion, the neighborhood watchmen scrutinize the comings and goings of all who live on their street, eagerly anticipating just one opportunity to blow the whistle on another. Can you imagine a neighborhood watchman with full view into the glass house of a leader?!

To my dismay, I have discovered that leaders sometimes serve as neighborhood watchmen on behalf of other leaders. A ministry leader and mentor to other leaders greatly struggled with an attitude of superiority. To remain in constant and complete control of others, the superior implemented methods of leadership which rewarded loyalty above integrity. In doing this, the superior leader aligned people under his authority who blindly yielded to the leader's plans and desires. In essence, the superior selected personal neighborhood watchmen to peruse and observe the leadership of other leaders within the organization.

In selecting specific individuals to serve as watchmen, the superior leader ascertained those who were simply and easily led. Manipulation, flattery, and the promise of rewards were common practices that enabled the leader to maintain complete loyalty from the watchmen. These watchmen were required to meet in secret, report, and assess the actions and motivations of other leaders within the ministry in which they all served together. Plainly said, the superior leader established a group of glorified tattle-tales within a God-formed organization.

Oh, dear leader, this approach to leadership causes us to lead our followers into deep sin. You see, the superior leader committed sin against his selected watchmen. He required judgment, secrecy, gossip, and disenfranchisement of fellow leaders. The leader committed sin against those being watched. Those who were watched were excluded, accused, evaluated, and betrayed by fellow leadership, their equals. The superior leader committed sin against followers in the ministry because of the poor example that was set by their leader.

Truth, honesty, and personal communication from us leaders to our followers are rashly discarded by these methods. This is an unacceptable example from leaders to followers! Such methods are solely rooted in paranoia and an obsession to control others. The motives are narcissistic and impure, and they must not be found in us leaders.

Effective leaders, exhibiting the qualities of integrity, sincerity, and transparency, must do all we can to avoid a deceitful approach to leading. Because we have been called to lead, have been given the honor to lead other leaders, and have been awarded the privilege of leading in the Body of Christ, we have **no excuse** to establish personal watchmen to assist our plans. Under no circumstances does the end justify the means here for us leaders. Simply said, people have been used! Leaders may never **use** people. This is not leadership. It is oppression, bondage, extortion, and servitude under the cloak of our God-given authority. These descriptions sound harsh, but they are complete truth.

If we find ourselves in such a devastating place as leaders, we must turn from it immediately! We must redefine God's intent for the watchman and adopt it as our own. Watchmen are chosen because they are keen, observant, and perceptive to the needs of others. We must appoint the watchmen whom God has given to assist us in protecting, guiding, nurturing, and leading others in the ways of the Lord. Watchmen are extensions of their leaders.

As leaders, let's pause and consider our watchmen. Are my helpers following the ways of God, and not mine, without reservation? Am I leading other leaders, equipping them to lead better than I myself, or do I desire superiority at any cost? Are my watchmen full of character, perseverance, and strength? Are their hearts and minds focused on God, meditating on His Word? Are the watchmen, along with me, leading by a godly example? Are they protecting, guiding, nurturing, and loving the flock unconditionally?

It is our responsibility as leaders for leaders to instill God's intentions and requirements for leadership within our watchmen. In turn, we must provide the resources and moral support for the watchmen to be successful — personally, spiritually, and ministerially. This process embodies leaders productively enabling leaders, one of which I hope to be a part!

A House Divided

*U*nless we leaders keep our hearts progressively pure, we will not remain in unity with God or others. Mishandling of our watchmen, sin, apathy, personal weaknesses, or denial that we are not the leader we should be destroy the unity in any ministry. I am certain that you have heard, "a house divided against itself cannot stand," (see Mark 3:25).

Many determine or define unity as keeping the peace, an absence of conflict, or all people thinking in the same way. Unfortunately, we leaders must see beyond these acceptable meanings of unity to its complete definition. Leadership does not allow us to accept the meaning of unity at face value. Leaders are also responsible to understand the deepest concepts of it.

Peace, no conflict, and sharing similar thoughts are valid results of unity, but they are not unity in and of themselves. Unity occurs when two or more things are so inter-twined that we cannot easily differentiate one from another. Unity is an unconditional, unrestrained merging of at least two into one. To accomplish unity, there is a minimum of two. Affirmative evidence proving unity is that the merger of two or more is, now, better than when they were separate. In continuum, endless results are possible due to unity.

To offer a clear understanding of unity, allow me to share an example of a leader's misunderstanding of it. A leader determined; it was time to establish a new program within his ministry. The program would directly benefit many and indirectly benefit some. While extremely useful and full of great potential, the new program would be quite costly. Because of the severity of it, financial and service commitments for the program would be required from many led by this leader.

Many were in complete favor of the program. Some were apprehensive to support it based on valid concerns of numerical and economical restraints. Leadership staff within this ministry also shared concerns about moving forward with the program within the set period of time. Leaders were in favor of the program, but they were not able to affirm the proper time to initiate it. Apprehensions of the followers and ministry staff alike infuriated the leader. This ignited a personal campaign on the part of the leader to aggressively address the principle of unity within the organization.

Misguided, the leader determined the meaning of unity to be that everyone in the organization shared the same thoughts. Unfortunately, those who thought differently were marked as those whose intent was to destroy the unity of the ministry. They were labeled as trouble-makers or conflict-causers. These people, followers and staff alike, were rebuked in public settings and belittled for their personal opinions. In the name of unity, this ministry house was divided by every harsh word that came from the lips of its leader. In a simple sentence of ill-spoken words, this leader moved from leader, to infuriated leader, to aggressive bully. We all know that bullies never bring together, but they always divide. Bullies intimidate and destroy.

As a leader, I am deeply saddened that we think a different way of thinking automatically means division or a lack of unity; that we must become defensive. We initiate a division of the people into groupings of those who are **for** and those who are **opposed.** This is unnecessary and is to be avoided. This poor attempt to establish unity motivates me to understand and grasp that I must be secure and confident in Christ as I lead His people.

In such a case, can unity be accomplished? Absolutely! Leaders, we deeply desire unity, but we must accept the responsibilities that accompany our leading in order to establish it. If the infuriated leader graciously accepted the different opinions of others, unity would have been accomplished. Naturally, all parties would not have been of the same thinking, but they would have been of the same mind. The program was needed and all spoke in its favor. While the program might have moved forward based on the majority of its supporters, the apprehensive would have been awarded their right to share concerns. In this, the two distinct groups have agreed to disagree. In reality, they have remained unified, since they have agreed on the same theory — disagreement without disenfranchisement.

Assuming that all parties would conduct themselves with graciousness and godliness, both would accept the work of the Lord being accomplished, regardless of the thinking of man. God pushes forward what He wants, and He holds back what He does not want. In complete unity, no words of anger or malice are spoken against another.

No campaigns or movements to choose sides are invoked, because unity remains intact; the unconditional, unrestrained merging of two or more into one, completely better to wholly serve the Lord.

As a leader, this lesson of unity resonates in my mind if others disagree with me, or they disagree with those I lead. I recall it when any threat comes against the unity in my marriage, my family, and my personal relationship with Christ. Remember, friends: Since leaders live in glass houses, others search for the absence of peace, constant conflict, and stubborn individuals continually fighting against each other to achieve their own way. Others clearly see the results caused by the lack of unity. Spectators search for unity within our homes and within our leadership. We must be passionate and dedicated to establish unity, combat the attacks against it, and realize the evidence which proves it is or is not there.

House Fire

*T*hroughout history, the burnings of great cities have been repeatedly reported. We have read of Sodom, Gomorrah, Jerusalem, Rome, and many others. Unfortunately, these great cities burned to rubble because of the wickedness of the people living within them. Repulsive, immoral behavior and crimes against mankind were noted as the typical lifestyle of those citizens. At some point, redemption seemed impossible for these horrific places, because their inhabitants refused to mend their ways of living.

Unfortunately, a catastrophic fire might engulf the glass house of a leader. If we have chosen to deny accountability, have become consumed with pride, have failed to remain in submission to the Holy Spirit, or have fallen to secret sin, a house fire is almost inevitable. If we leaders have separated ourselves from the authority of God in our leadership, we replace His authority with complete autonomy. Something must be done for God to regain our attention. The severity of our sin and separation determines the severity of His methods used to bring us to our humble knees before God.

Oh, leader, we must do everything in our power to mend our ways before God and others. Understand the devastation of any house fire. Whether just one room or the entire house is consumed to ashes and soot, the impact is the same. Fear comes to anyone near or entrapped in a fire. Smoke and toxic fumes are as destructive as the heat and flames themselves. Fire moves quickly and burns hotter as it travels. Everything in its path becomes black. Debris left behind needs attention. It is extremely costly to repair or replace anything damaged by fire, smoke, soot, water, or fire extinguisher.

When deep, hidden sin dwells and grows within our leaders' hearts, a spark is ignited for personal and leadership destruction. Any small, unconfessed sin can culminate into the heart and life of a leader, causing him to be completely consumed and blackened by it. With God, all sins are equal. The level of impact or measure of others hurt by sin carries the degree of its effect. The more people who are negatively affected by our sin, the greater the level of damage that is done. Additionally, deeper consequences fall upon us leaders.

It is very easy for leaders to sin. It is very challenging for leaders to be holy in our leadership. It is very easy for leaders to take the path of least resistance; so therefore, we yield to personal desires and will. We fall into the trap of thinking, "One small sin can go unnoticed. No one will find out." The end justifies the means, for this one time. We might often mislead others to condone our sin, distorting and twisting our explanation of it to seem as if we are fighting against "true" evil. With each twist and turn, the spaces and walls of our glass house fill with the smoke and fire of sin. Black clouds billow high within, removing all signs of a pure life.

Satan attacks the home and life of the effective, godly leader. He is so desperate to find the smallest place in which to ignite the spark of sin, and then he waits and watches the fire burn as quickly as possible. The more lives consumed, the more casualties resulting, the more Satan is pleased.

As children, we were taught by our parents and teachers that we must not play with matches or fire. Our leaders hoped we would grasp that such a small thing was so dangerous, and it could cause tremendous damage in spite of its size. Our warnings concerning fire came regularly and with determination.

Please, leaders! May we commit and join together to run from the matches, the sparks of deep, dark sin. We all sin, daily as it may, but our sin has been, is, and will be conquered and overpowered if the Holy Spirit is in complete control of our hearts. Sin is the conqueror and overpowers us when **we** are in complete control.

Since we leaders live in glass houses, others see the result and destruction from a fire very quickly. It is quite obvious that, if all the glass is blackened, something horrible has occurred inside. Something took place inside one of our houses, and there was no stopping it in time. The question may be asked, "Did anyone survive?" Assumptions are made concerning the casualties. Those who pass by and are unable to see clearly will continue on their way, not looking back or returning. You see, if our lives are consumed by sin, others will refuse to follow us leaders. They determine that we will lead them incorrectly.

As leaders worthy to be followed, we must practice safety drills daily, galvanizing ourselves through prayer and Bible study. Safety measures must be activated to warn us of Satan's attempts to infiltrate with sin and ignite the destruction of a house fire. We must humbly request that our peer leaders, prayer warriors, and dedicated saints pray diligently for our protection in this area. Sin is serious and disabling; we cannot risk losing the hearts and souls of those we lead to die in the ashes from our sin. We leaders must remain humble, confess sin, repent, and defy sin's return to our hearts and lives. Remember; priceless valuables may be completely destroyed and unable to be replaced due to fire. Are they worth the risk?

Without Power

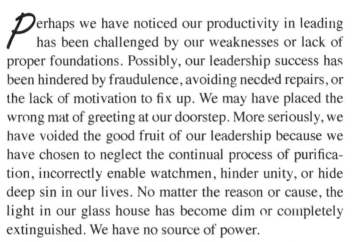

*P*erhaps we have noticed our productivity in leading has been challenged by our weaknesses or lack of proper foundations. Possibly, our leadership success has been hindered by fraudulence, avoiding needed repairs, or the lack of motivation to fix up. We may have placed the wrong mat of greeting at our doorstep. More seriously, we have voided the good fruit of our leadership because we have chosen to neglect the continual process of purification, incorrectly enable watchmen, hinder unity, or hide deep sin in our lives. No matter the reason or cause, the light in our glass house has become dim or completely extinguished. We have no source of power.

Remaining connected to our Power Source is a massive expectation for any leader. In our literal home, the uninterrupted flowing of power allows things to function properly, from **the necessities** like: using the lights, to cooling the refrigerator, to heating the water, to cooking on the stove, or to laundering the clothes. It also allows proper functioning of **the desired** within the home like: watching television, to playing video games, to using power tools, to charging cell phones, or to using air conditioners.

Connection to a power source is vital for use, and connection to our Power Source is vital for our use as a leader.

There are times the items that we use may have their switches in the **off** position, but they remain plugged in to their source of power. The minute we unplug a power cord, there is no hope of us getting any use from it. If a cord remains plugged in, with the simple flipping of its switch, we can receive its benefits. This may seem like such a childish example for us leaders, but it carries an extremely adult lesson. A leader must remain connected, at all times, to God, our complete Power Source.

Any number of challenges or struggles can pull and tug against our hearts and minds. With all heart and effort, we must do everything possible to remain connected to the Lord. Little things may lean hard against us, moving us into that **off position,** but if we are diligent to stay connected to our Power Source, God can easily return us to full and productive use. Occasionally, minimal time in an **off position** may give us needed relief or prevent us from over-heating (losing control) as a leader. In earnest, there should never be a desire within us leaders to disconnect from the power of the Lord.

Obviously, improper disconnection or a faulty power connection can be the unstoppable spark that causes a house fire. After this fire, it is impossible to see light in the incinerated, blackened home. It will require rebuilding, replacing power connections, and returning to the Power Source for us to shine our Light.

If we find ourselves completely disconnected from the power of the Lord, two things occur. We are either without power and use, or we are running on our own power and by our own use. Both are detrimental to any success and productivity of a leader. It is paramount that we immediately determine our cause for disconnection and restore it. Power from the wrong source can cause the dimming of a light; therefore, its illumination is quite limited or none at all. This principle is applicable to all leaders attempting to be their own source of power. Our man-powered light of leadership causes our followers to strain their eyes and stumble due to our lack of proper power. Darkness is imminent. Confusion is probable.

Practically stated, we are the first to enter a dark room, and we turn on the light. As others follow behind, we have ensured their clear visibility and unobstructed path to entering the room safely, because we have turned on a light. We have also ensured our easy passage. We would never think of turning on a light, entering a room, and then turning off the light, because we have stepped inside the room. In this, we have set ourselves up to stumble and fall, perhaps breaking a body part.

Likewise, we would never think of turning on a light, entering a room with others following behind us, and then turning off the light because everyone stepped inside the room. Not only would this be a cruel joke of sorts; we would cause all those who followed us to stumble, fall, break body parts, or hurt others, because no one could find their way.

While my example may seem absurd, since we leaders would never lead in such a way, it can occur if we refuse to rely on the Lord as our ultimate Source of power in our leadership. We must keep in mind the results that can hinder or hurt our followers due to our lack of power. In addition, we cannot see clearly ourselves in order to lead others. The lack of power affects us as well. We are blinded, misguided leaders.

Staying connected to the Lord, uninterrupted, through our personal relationship with Him, is a proactive process. In being the first to enter a room and turn on the light, we are proactive leaders. The room is now well-lit and safe for others to enter.

We leaders must not adopt a reactive approach to leading when having the power of the Lord in our leadership. This can be shown in such an example as: Followers enter a dark room. They stumble, inadvertently push others, complain of the darkness, and fall. In reaction, the leader turns on the light, after the damage has already occurred. In reaction, assessments of casualties must be made by the leader. In reaction, help must be given to those who have hurt themselves because they were unable to see. The leader did not act beforehand, but they reacted afterwards.

Please understand, there will be numerous times throughout our leadership when we cannot see all things coming. If we were able to determine every possible scenario, outcome, and person within our tenure of leadership, we could be called gods, indeed. As power-filled leaders, we must adopt a proactive approach to leadership, at least attempting to set others up for success. At times, reaction is necessary and effective in the power of the Lord. Only God knows in advance what we will face as leaders. If we remain connected to Him, we leaders are most proactive, less reactive, and rarely having to perform damage-control for things gone wrong.

Dear leader, we must remain in an uninterrupted connection to our Power Source. Because our houses are made of glass, light can very easily be seen. We must grasp tightly to the Word of God which allows us to be seen, within our houses and beyond, as leaders of Light.

New Paint

*O*ver time, the paint of the interior or the exterior of our home begins to fade. The fading and tainting may come from over-exposure to the elements, routine wear-and-tear, or extreme abuse that comes with even the happiest of times in our home. No matter when we take notice of the paint's dingy appearance, we immediately realize that it is time to do something about it. It is time for new paint!

A paint job requires that a few important details be determined before any new paint is applied. First, the surface to be painted must be properly prepared so the new coat of paint is able to adhere to it. This may mean some rough scraping and abrasive sanding to remove any remnant of the withered, peeling paint from its original application. I know I have had to use a brush made with steel bristles, occasionally, to smooth away old paint chips that refused to loosen themselves. The surface must be thoroughly cleaned. An application of primer may be needed, particularly if old paint has been completely stripped away. Finally, we can move on to the next step for painting.

Now, we must decide on the color and type of the new paint. We must consider questions such as: How long do I expect this paint to endure? What finish do I desire from it? Is it soluble to certain chemicals? Am I looking for the same result as the old paint, or do I hope for a different result? Is this paint easy to change if I find I was not wise in choosing it?

Lastly, we must compare the new paint selection with the colors of the items which remain in proximity to it. For the exterior of our home, we must consider the current color of the doors, shutters, and trim. Regarding the interior, we must consider the existing furniture and decorative accessories. We also compare other painted walls that connect to those which we desire to repaint. We may be as thorough as to consider whether or not the new paint color fits properly into the theme and mood of our decorative genius. Nonetheless, new paint cannot be applied until a process has been followed and our questions have been answered.

Our motivation for applying new paint to any surface is so that its recipient will look improved, attractive, and as if it is brand new. Our desire is to invest a fair amount of time in applying the paint now, so our enjoyment of it will last many times longer than the hours it took us to do the work. Our hope is that the new paint covers flaws and presents a refreshing appearance to anyone who sees it. Our joy is found over time if the new paint benefits us far longer than we expected by sealing, protecting, and withstanding any destructive elements.

In leadership, we can become dingy, withered, and peeling away after harsh exposure to certain elements. Everyday wear-and-tear on us leaders can fade or taint us, so we might appear unattractive to others. In times of hardship or distress within our leadership role, we might feel somewhat over-used or abused, losing our true brightness and color. It is, indeed, time to receive a new coat of paint. It is time for change!

Some leaders take much longer than others to recognize our need for improvement. It may take the figurative scraping and abrasion to enlighten and inspire us to apply something new to our leadership. I do believe that if things are working well, do not be too quick to change them. I also believe that good changes have a very positive impact on our leadership methods and style.

In making changes that affect not only us, but those who follow our leadership, it is of greatest importance that we consider the result we desire to accomplish through our changes. Effective leaders determine and evaluate how easily change comes to those who follow us. We consider the potential outcome as much as possible when preparing to make a change.

Change is inevitable in life. It is inevitable in people, and it is inevitable in leadership as well. There is a need for change. It is determined based on the leader, our followers, and the circumstances surrounding us. The crux of the matter is the manner in which we leaders apply the changes. As with a brush smoothing paint on a wall, so a leader must apply changes evenly, smoothly, and with the proper amount of pressure. This is the only method of application that is followed with a successful, beautiful result.

The leader who chooses to apply changes with force or in excessive amounts will find the result spotted and skewed. There is no balance for followers who must accept changes that are forced upon them without proper preparation. We leaders do not always handle changes forced upon us with grace and maturity. We cannot expect those who follow to accept rash changes easily, either. A leader does have the authority to make changes and adjustments on behalf of those whom we lead; however, the proper steps of preparation must be taken prior to the changes. The better people are informed of forthcoming changes, the easier they will accept them. Integrity, sincerity, and transparency are vital here.

This takes us leaders to our final caution in making needed changes. Just as we compare and determine the compatibility of any new paint to the items in its proximity, so we compare new items for change with the people that will be affected by them. We may easily see our need to change an aspect of our leadership style or methods. We may be very willing to implement new ideas or strategies for ministry, but an open-minded, listening leader is one who is viewed as approachable and not intimidating to those who are apprehensive of change. Our listening assists our followers to make changes without reservation.

Leaders who make changes that do not fit the intended recipients of change cause great harm. We must consider a leader of a school. The newly assigned leader to the school's administrative position determined that the school was in great need of authoritative, structural changes. The leader's approach was to change the job descriptions and requirements of all leaders within the school. Full authority previously given to some was revoked, while ambiguous guidelines for more authority were given to others. Harsh mandates were placed upon staff, students, and parents. Severe consequences were threatened for any who chose not to comply. Ultimatums were served and followed with threats of unemployment.

Inconsistency in communicating details of the changes proved routinely evident. Confusion overtook adults and students alike. No one understood the changes that occurred one day and then seemed to be retracted the next. This leader was so intensely motivated to apply changes and to be the authority that he never considered the proper preparation to initiate his changes. The leader never evaluated the recipients of change, and never considered the potential outcome of his changes. The changes did not fit the followers, and the followers did not fit the changes! Regretfully, the leader disregarded the mandates of his own regulatory changes, issuing self-exemption. Integrity, sincerity, and transparency were noticeably extinct and caused nothing but a clash of wills.

It is to be expected that this high-pressure, inconsiderate approach to making changes failed miserably. The leader could not maintain integrity; he could not remain consistent. He could not maintain consistency, since he had not performed the proper preparation to begin the process for applying changes. The changes did not take place effectively because the leader failed to determine if the changes were appropriate for the designated group of followers.

Understandably, some people take far longer than others to accept changes as good things. If **God** is directing our thoughts and actions as leaders, the changes prove themselves positive, beneficial, and appropriate. There is little opposition to God-directed changes, and unity remains as they are made. A smooth application occurs with successful and beautiful results.

As viewers sit back and observe the changes we make in ourselves and within our ministries, they scope to see our successes or failures. Our glass houses are a clear give-away of the true colors that paint our leadership. We must take adequate time and be patient as leaders to follow a successful process for making changes. God always pre-pares the hearts of the people for the plan that He has in mind. He makes our followers ready to receive and be improved by the changes which He guides us to apply.

We leaders must allow those peering inside our houses of glass to see that we are willing to make changes as needed, in our personal lives and in our leadership. People must see we are patiently applying the process. In essence, we seem to be waiting for one coat of paint to dry before attempting to apply another. People must see us leaders taking the time to ensure that our changes will improve and preserve them. Others must also see us making only God's intended changes. If our changes have been detri-mental, harmful, and unsuccessful, as in the leadership of the school, we must admit our wrong-doing as leaders, and we must correct it. If the **paint** we selected is the wrong color, we must recognize it; admit it, and exchange it as efficiently as possible. Dwelling in the glass house requires clarity, so others may see our best colors!

Curb Appeal

To any home buyer or seller, the curb appeal of a home is a top priority. Curb appeal is the distinct first impression that a home makes on its potential buyer. If a home has a well-groomed lawn, neatly arranged, weed-free flower beds, and a nicely decorated front door, the house draws any potential buyer to look inside it. The assumption is that if it looks so presentable on the outside, the inside is guaranteed to impress. This leads to the success of the home sale, which benefits the buyer and the seller.

Contrariwise, for a potential buyer to approach a home with uncut grass, over-grown weeds, and a dirty front door, the buyer does not consider looking any further into the home. A very poor first impression is given to the buyer. If the buyer is courageous enough to look inside this house, he approaches it with great caution and reservation, having very low expectations of seeing anything good inside it. This leads to the failure of the home sale, which discourages the buyer and the seller.

In today's world of leadership, leaders must impress. Whether we like this expectation or we do not, it **does** affect the outcome of our leadership. It is so important that we understand **why** we must impress and **how** to impress. In making a godly impression, our leadership appeals to others; God is proven to them through us.

While personality traits such as enthusiasm, charisma, and extroversion are profitable in connecting with people, a leader who takes a quiet, subtle approach to connecting does not lack appeal. God created each of us with a different personality, employing diverse traits to reach as many people as possible. Remember; Jesus took the same approach when He called His twelve different disciples. They were not all determined go-getters or sympathetic softies.

In spite of personality distinctions, we leaders have qualities that appeal to those we lead. God works through our specific personalities to make impressions on specific people, therefore allowing us to appeal to them. When we appeal to those we lead, they willingly submit to and respect our leadership. When followers submit to and respect our leadership, we can lead them in the ways of God. God becomes real in their lives, because they trust us to lead them to Him. They trust us, since we have impressed them; and our leadership appeals to them. This is **why** we must impress as leaders.

We may not allow ourselves to hinder making a positive impression for the Lord. We cannot be motivated to impress others; hoping to appeal to them so they think that we are wonderful. We cannot desire to be so impressive and appealing to people as their leaders that our pride blocks a clear view of God, our Leader. We must keep our feet on the ground and our heads out of the clouds, understanding that God alone allows us to be impressive and appealing for His good pleasure.

As leaders, we understand that we are to impress for God's glory. We are not called to please people. Remember my foundation mentioned earlier? **Distinguish personal preferences from biblical convictions.** If we attempt to please others through leadership, we lead for the praises of man and not the glory of God. We lead for all that we can gain and offer nothing of substance to people or the Lord. We lead for power and authority and never yield in humility. We must stop this process before it even starts!

How we impress fuses from the heart within us as leaders to the evidence which is seen without by followers. Integrity, sincerity, and transparency must engulf our character and describe our leadership. Clear acceptance and understanding of God's requirements for His leaders is necessary. Taking responsibility and living in righteousness as a leader is non-compromising. Leading and living under accountability is without question!

Impressive, godly leaders with appeal are respected, admired, loved, and easily followed by others. Those who follow us feel at ease and know that they will benefit from our instruction. We live what we teach. We walk the walk ourselves and do not just talk the talk in front of our followers.

This type of leader recognizes that, while he has been given authority by his calling, he yields to the accountability of others. No matter the level of leadership in which we find ourselves, we leaders remain accountable to someone. A leader is accountable to his godly peers. We are accountable to society's leaders, such as law and government. Obviously, we are always accountable to Almighty God, but we are also accountable to those we lead. We **do** have to answer to and for them regarding our godly, or ungodly, leadership which affects them.

Do you desire to be a remarkably impressive and appealing leader who is tremendously effective? Ask the people you lead to hold you accountable to godliness in your life and leadership, because **they** are worthy of it. Be humble enough to receive it. The response and result will be earth-shaking! We gain immeasurable respect as leaders when we accept the responsibility to lead, yet consider ourselves as one who follows. We are approachable while having authority. This type of leader impresses and appeals to all who follow him. It will be said, "How impressive is our leader!" Our glass house will shine to the stars and be long-remembered.

Equally stated, do you desire to fail to impress and be unappealing as a tremendously ineffective leader? Ask for no accountability, and make excuses as to why no one is capable of holding you to it. Remain prideful, and reject it. Complain about the immaturity of those who follow you. The response and result will be glass-shattering! We gain no respect as leaders when we feel we are above those who follow us. This type of leader is arrogant and unappealing to all who follow him. We are defensive and argumentative. It will be said, "How oppressive is our leader!" Our glass house will shatter to dust and be infamously remembered.

Growing Pains

*F*rom the moment we are born, we begin to grow. We grow up; we grow out of, and into things. We pass through stages, taking us from one growth plateau to the next. While people grow at various rates, we all move through the same progressive stages for development.

As leaders, we all grow. We pass through stages, grow at various rates, grow out of and into things, and grow up. The healthy growth rate of a leader is one that positively enables him while positively developing those who follow him. We cannot deny; we will experience growing pains throughout the stages of our growth.

What might we as leaders **grow out of?** When we are initially called to leadership, we may experience emotions and thoughts reaching from both ends of the spectrum. We may feel completely overwhelmed, under-developed, and fearful. We may also think we have finally arrived to our well-deserved seat of appointment. Whichever the thought, either perspective of oneself in leadership is immature.

We must out-grow the idea that because we are called to leadership, we have nothing more to learn. While God equips us with gifts for leadership, He gives us minds to learn. As we become leaders, we do not instantaneously **know it all.** Parents can well-relate to this attitude which often appears in our children. When they become eighteen, legal adult age, our children instantaneously think, "I know it all!" As the growing pains of life lessons came to us at that age and come to our children as they grow, they also come to leaders who refuse to out-grow a distorted perspective of our leadership.

What might we as leaders **grow into**? As we grew up, we recall the permissiveness, or lack thereof, from our parents. As we competently handled one aspect of the growth process, another was initiated or permitted. Upon mastery of preliminary concepts, new concepts were taught and practiced. Perhaps curfews were extended. Responsibilities were added, and liberties increased as we accomplished each prerequisite properly. Sometimes these lessons brought with them a bit of pain or challenge.

So it is with a leader. As a growing baby moves from the infant seat, to the highchair, to the booster seat, to the dining room chair, we move from seat to seat of responsibility as God sees our mastery from one concept of our leadership to another. We must adequately grow into leaders that can competently apply God's lessons, hand-crafted uniquely for us and our growth rate. We must first adequately fit into one seat so we can move into the next for additional growth.

How might we as leaders **grow up**? Over time, through experience, through the guidance of the Scriptures, and by God's blessings, we grow up. Each day of leadership offers the experience and instruction which allow us to have a steady, developmental growth rate in leading others. This process of maturing occurs in our physical bodies, our mental minds, and our emotional growth. It occurs in our spiritual souls as we seek the Lord. Lastly, it occurs in our leadership as we submit to our Holy God. The result is His growing of us. We grow up; we mature.

During extended growth periods, the pains of growing are more intense and harder to bear than at other times. When we learned to walk, we fell. When we fell, we hurt. When we hurt, we cried. Miraculously, we attempted to walk again; we instinctively knew we would be so much better-off if we walked. In spite of the pain and its hurtful cycle, we repeated this process of growing until we had the victory — **freedom of movement on our own.** Maturity was accomplished.

Any leader must grow at God's determined rate of progression and not his own. If we are faithful to endure each stage in spite of its level of growing pain, we maintain a healthy growth rate in our leadership. Leaders, we never master every lesson for growing in our leadership the first time in which it presents itself. If we do not fully succeed, we try again until we achieve. Our followers may or may not be aware of the growth we are making as it is happening, but they will certainly reap the full benefits of our growth. Here is where we become positively enabled, and here is where our followers become positively developed due to our enabling. We can do it! We can grow to maturity.

Regretfully, we must consider leaders who **refuse to grow up.** The leader who will not grow out of a certain stage in leadership development should be objectively considered by his followers. Should others really continue to follow us? All things should be completely considered when it comes to being a leader of the Lord's flock. Our followers have the right to refuse to follow us if we are not capable to lead.

A micro-managing leader is immature. Refusing to relinquish control to anyone other than ourselves is immature. Constructing figurative walls of defense and viewing ourselves as perpetual victims of attack is immature. Intending to damage the reputations of others so they look bad and we look good is immature. The "I'll show them," approach is immature. Losing control of our tempers, our speech, and our actions is immature. If we are these leaders, we refuse to grow up! In true reality, we should not be leading others until we have mastered control of this developmental stage. There are no reasonable excuses for it.

In full balance, a leader who refuses to grow into required aspects and actions of leadership should also be objectively considered by his followers. Avoiding necessary, difficult decisions in our leadership displays our failure to grow. Rejecting increased accountability as the number of those following increases displays a great failure to grow. Desiring the privileges that come with greater leadership but denying the responsibilities which accompany it displays our failure to grow. Seeking the title and accolades of leadership and despising the mandates of humility and servitude displays our failure to grow.

If we are these leaders, we choose to remain in the less demanding stages of leadership. We refuse to grow into mature leaders in Christ. In true reality, we must tightly grasp hold of accountability and the assistance of a wiser, godly mentor to steadily help us grow through this developmental stage of our leadership. Refusal to do so may result in our potential removal from leadership and a detrimental disabling of the dear saints who follow us.

If we are proper leaders, it is obvious to others that our intention is to grow. Those who follow continuously witness our best efforts to grow out of immature leadership, grow into mature leadership, and grow up to maturity as their leaders. If we make continual attempts to better ourselves as leaders, patience and understanding readily come from our followers, in spite of our failed first-attempts or misses. If we have established our integrity, sincerity, and transparency as effective leaders, followers are gracious and accepting of the fact; even leaders need time and space in which to grow. They exhibit the understanding that if their leader is growing properly, they benefit from his growth.

Oh, dear leader! We must come to grips with the honest desire of our hearts at this point. Do we desire to lead God's way through integrity, sincerity, and transparency? Do we understand that this marvelous call of God to lead came because He requires us to wholly follow Him as we lead others? We must examine our hearts. We must humble ourselves and admit our failures. We must confess our sin and make wrongs right. We must decide to improve ourselves and grow toward maturity in our leadership, or we must courageously admit that we are not yet ready or worthy to lead.

As effective leaders, we must be well aware of anything that may threaten or stunt our growth process. We must face these hurdles with mature courage and tenacity. We must determine to grow properly in order to dwell in the glass house and obtain full understanding of God's reason for it. We must, indeed, be worthy of this dwelling place.

Septic Tank

─────※─────

*W*e will never clearly see or comprehend God's intentions for our glass house if we have failed to grow or have chosen to sink into the muck and mire of personal filth. We would not be complete in our thoughts and responsibilities as leaders if we did not consider the repulsive, dirty side of leadership that might occur in today's world. We leaders cannot deny the existence of such practices and qualities that should only result in complete removal from leadership ministry. In warning, these characterizations are disgusting, repulsive, and infuriating. Any leader should be well-motivated to avoid them. Any follower should be well-informed to avoid following the leader that fits these descriptions.

Sewage Pipe #1: **Tyranny**- Today is not the age of Napoleon or the generation of Hitler. It is not within the boundaries of our leadership to require any level of compliance from our followers. It is not the right of us leaders to facilitate **the Mob** approach to leadership. A tyrannical mob leader requires submission from followers through oppression, and he threatens consequences upon those who refuse to submit. A non-compliant must be kept quiet at all costs. This could mean one's removal from the tasks of which they are assigned, termination of employment, intimidation, or degradation of character. The tyrant poses threats, concocts evidence, avoids truth, and sends personal thugs to silence a follower's reasons for lack of submission. This leader has fallen into the sewage pipe of tyranny and is not worthy of authority, whether God-appointed, self-appointed, or appointed by others. In today's terms, this leader is a **bully**!

I once knew of a tyrannical leader who may serve as an example for us. This leader established a force of bodyguards. These guards had the responsibility of escorting their leader to all ministry events. The leader used intimidation, with the security officers serving as a tool, to send a clear message that no one dare attempt standing against nor approaching him.

Leaders who lead small-town ministries, are not nationally or internationally known, and have never led in community, civil, or political movements have no need for security protection. This leader definitely sent a clear message: "I am completely unapproachable and think very highly of myself! Bodyguards protect me from the Body of Christ, since I am superior. You can't touch me!" Where is the example of humility and hospitality from this leader? Where is the display of faith from the leader to the followers that God always protects us? Intimidating **mob** leadership is ridiculous, unacceptable, and a show of pomp and pride. In the least, bodyguards should be protecting and guarding the hearts of the Body of Christ!

Sewage Pipe #2: **Smooth Talking**- Manipulation of word meanings and the context in which words are spoken is the smooth-talking leader's method of accomplishing personal agendas and suppressing the intelligent minds of his followers. Leaders characterized by smooth talking are likened to society's definition of a *slimy politician*. This leader answers questions with questions. After a futile exchange of questions within a conversation, the leader causes the follower to become confused, feel inferior, and lose confidence in himself. A smooth-talking leader manipulates the mind and words of the one following, so much that the follower cannot recall their need to question the leader in the first place. This is not the practice of reflective listening, for the reiterated questions are never completely true to their originals. This leader has fallen into the sewage pipe of smooth talking and is not worthy of instructing followers.

An illustration of a smooth-talking leader lies within the practices of a leader whom I once observed. The leader had an authoritative board in addition to his own leadership authority. Routinely, this leader communicated to the board of his willingness to yield to the final decisions and rulings of the board. The leader only presented issues or items of no concern to their board. It was irrelevant to the leader if the items went forward or were rejected by the authority of the board. The items were insignificant.

Decisions of weight and importance were made only by the leader. Since the leader so smoothly communicated of his willingness to submit to the board, the board never recognized the deceit and manipulation taking place. The board believed they had complete authority, which was slyly conveyed by this smooth-talking leader.

Sewage Pipe #3: **Biblical Balderdash.** Biblical balderdash is nothing but misguidance and deception. It is an inaccurate use of the Scriptures by a leader upon a follower through which to achieve the leader's desired result. It may appear in the form of a biblical lesson, policy, or sermon, but Scripture is withdrawn from its context and inspired meaning. It is distorted by a leader to inflict guilt, fear, or control upon those who follow. Biblical balderdash is synonymous with false teaching, therefore making a leader a false teacher or false leader. It does not coincide with the biblical doctrine which is to govern our lives. This leader has fallen deeply into the sewage pipe of biblical balderdash and is not worthy to impart biblical teaching to those who follow him.

In my college days, I experienced biblical balderdash from a leader of some form within my life. I was dating a "preacher boy," as students training for pastoral ministry were often called, prior to meeting my wonderful husband. The young man was determined to debate with anyone about any topic of biblical meaning.

One day, the topic of the biblical roles of men and women was presented. The preacher boy had very definitive ideas and opinions about the subject. He repeatedly stated the role of women is in submission and subjection to men, the leaders. Even within an uninvolved, dating relationship, the young man felt all biblical principles of male leadership applied. Using his biblical balderdash, he gave me instructions concerning what to wear, ways to style my hair, to whom I could speak, the types of sports in which I could participate, and the list goes on. His use of the Word of God was inaccurate, false, distorted, and used to gain control. Obviously, we never married!

Sewage Pipe #4: **Bait and Tackle.** This method of leadership is destructive and divisive. A leader and their personally chosen minions maintain separation between members in a ministry or organization. Collaboration by anyone other than these leaders is forbidden. This leader sets bait, hoping to gain the naïve trust of one following. The trust is then used to gain information or material which benefits the leader's intents. Bait is also set to entrap another, therefore giving a leader the ammunition necessary to destroy or eliminate another. In essence, this is an ambush. The motivation behind it is sabotage of the saints, hoping for an end result of division and vulnerability for conquering. The leader who has fallen into the sewage pipe of bait and tackle will, at some point, become entangled in his own trap, justifiably!

An experience of bait and tackle became reality when an athlete did not care for the coach of his team. As a leader of wrong-doing and harm against others, the athlete presented his reasons for removal of the coach. He secretly questioned team members, posing leading statements such as, "Have you ever heard the coach say...*this* word?" "Did it look to you like the coach...did *this*?" With every question, the athlete led other team members to offer bits and pieces of information which could be manipulated into a strategic formation to use as an ambush for removing the coach. This disappointing leader solicited the trust of his team members to gain ambiguous information, intending to destroy another; baiting in order to tackle.

Sewage Pipe #5: **Perks.** Some leaders feel we are entitled to numerous perks and excessive expense accounts. The leader who takes the family to dinner at a popular restaurant, invites a friend from within the organization, and submits the dinner receipt for reimbursement, has taken unethical advantage of the financial donations given to the ministry. Because the leader invited another member to the meal, it does not justify the cost as a ministry expense.

The leader that purchases new shoes since they have worn out an old pair crossing a lengthy parking lot to the office each day may not expect the organization to pay for the new pair. Federal and tax regulations have been established for the use of ministry and organizational funds. It is the responsibility of us leaders to know the laws and abide by them without question.

Unethical leadership perks correlate with immoral leadership practices. The two go hand-in-hand. Ultimately, they often lead to theft, adultery, addictions, or much worse. The leader pursuing perks for personal enjoyment, to appear generous, or to gain social status has fallen into the sewage pipe of probable no return.

A devastating example of the corruption by perks for leaders provides us proof. A large ministry leader found it necessary to work in close proximity with a few members of their organization. Demands of the leadership position required long hours, consultation sessions, and joint leadership with others; all of which required collaboration with mixed genders. Think-tanks, group prayer times, and collective problem-solving were normal practices.

Through this environment, the leader developed mental, emotional, and physical ties to someone other than his spouse. When the adultery was discovered, the leader's rationale was that God brought another remarkable person into his life by way of the ministry; therefore, the leader knew he was meant to be with the new person. The leader continued that God had clearly **given** the new person to him, so he knew it was time to divorce the first. The leader implied a perk of leadership is that God speaks directly to leaders. God would never approve of such perversion in leadership!

It sickens and saddens me that this cesspool of leadership must be exposed. The filth of the septic tank lies within its contents of bacteria, infection, contamination, and parasites. Picturing all of these undesirable, unhealthy components, we leaders must be fearful of falling into the sewage pipes leading to this tank.

A candid comparison might be within the context of parental guidance for a small child. The child goes outdoors, entering the backyard. The child proceeds to play and takes little care of the yard. Within minutes, the child has tightly grasped a huge pile of animal excrement in his hand and is placing it in his mouth. In horror, the parent screams to warn the child not to ingest the disgusting parasites of filth that will contaminate his impressionable, little body. Once ingested, the feces will cause serious illness to come to the child for an undetermined period of time. If the child happens to touch another while still contaminated, the other will also become ill due to the infectious spreading of bacteria and parasites.

Leaders, please pardon my grotesque example, but take heed! We must acknowledge the existence of filth that can potentially spread through our leadership in literal minutes. I would be deeply amiss to deny that leadership is indeed a fight **for** purity and **against** impurity. If a septic tank overflows, the clean-up, decontamination, and emptying out of it requires extensive, unpleasant overhaul, as well as a great expense. Leaders cannot risk the stench and soiling within our God-given glass houses. One cannot predict the extent of the infection and contamination, not to mention the casualties that fall because of it.

Windowpanes

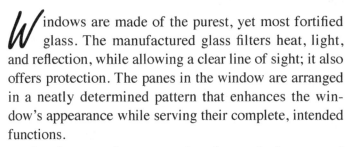

*W*indows are made of the purest, yet most fortified glass. The manufactured glass filters heat, light, and reflection, while allowing a clear line of sight; it also offers protection. The panes in the window are arranged in a neatly determined pattern that enhances the window's appearance while serving their complete, intended functions.

Leaders may be compared to the precisely arranged panes of a window. In our world today, there are many different leaders. All leaders form a complete body of leadership. Age, gender, life experience, and learned knowledge describe these leaders, but they do not necessarily define them all conclusively. You see; it has been said that leadership is influence. As many glass panes ultimately form one window, many types of leaders ultimately form our idea of influential leadership.

The father who holds his first-born baby in his arms has become a leader. The three-year-old boy who has just received his baby sister has become a leader. The high school junior who has been selected as captain of her soccer team has become a leader. The spokesperson for the college group presentation has become a leader. The newly appointed assistant to the town mayor has become a leader. Our list of examples may vary and continue, but this remains consistent: people have the potential to become leaders. All leaders have the opportunity to influence others.

In some cases, whether we desire it or not, we find ourselves leading others. The moment one becomes a parent, he influences the children in his home. While the little boy is only three, he has been granted the opportunity to influence his baby sister, simply because he was born first. Children, teenagers, and adults alike have influence upon others, regardless of how they have received their leadership roles.

Notice: I previously stated that leadership is influence. I have not yet specified the **kind** of leadership and the **kind** of influence. Just as the analogy is used that an apple tree will only bear apples, **one kind** of leadership only reproduces the **same kind** of influence. If we look into a glass windowpane, we see only our own reflection. I could never look into the glass and see the reflection of my husband. It is me and me alone!

Another common comparison made in identifying the true hearts of people is that **our behavior is the mirror of our soul.** If we conjoin the two concepts — leadership is influence, and our behavior is the mirror of our soul — we can conclude that our behavior determines our leadership influence, and our leadership influence displays our true soul.

Within the marriage of these two thoughts, we discover the **kind** of leadership and the **kind** of influence. To explain, the **rotten** leader has rotten behavior, yielding rotten influence, and revealing a rotten soul. A concrete example of the process lies within a basket of apples. One rotten apple in a basket decays, causing the other apples in the basket to decay as well. We will never find a rotten apple in a basket, leave it there, and then find that all the good apples have made the rotten one good. **Rotten** leadership yields rotten influence, which yields rotten followers.

In contrast, the **pure** leader has pure behavior, yielding pure influence, revealing a pure soul. Pure leadership yields pure influence, which yields pure followers. A second concrete example is that a good apple, placed in a basket of other good apples, will keep all apples good. But beware! A good apple, placed in a basket of rotten apples, will eventually become rotten; so get out, whether you are the leader or the follower!

As glass reflects only the original image, the influence of the leader reflects only the original leader. We must realize, leaders, that others witness our reflection, brightly and clearly. As we have been assigned and precisely arranged as God's windowpanes of leadership, we must never neglect the importance of the true image of our influence. Not only does the image display our true souls, it is also the method of assessment by which others determine if we are good leaders or rotten ones. Because our houses are made of glass, it is only appropriate that God would permit our followers to see into the windows of our souls as we lead.

Home Sweet *Glass* Home

*F*or the duration of our leadership term, we dwell in our glass houses. We have considered many obstacles, hindrances, and challenges that face us within it. So often, we push through the hard times and rarely enjoy the blessed times. If we are completely honest as leaders, I am sure we all question God's intention and purpose for us dwelling in these particular homes. We, most often, regard them with misery. We view them with resentment or as a sentence of punishment, because we have followed our call to lead. As a leader, how should I view this God-appointed home?

As I stated in previous chapters, God affirmed for me His purpose for my glass house just a few years ago. What must I do with this house? His answer: **Embrace it!** Yes, dear leader, embrace it! Remember; we are **called** to abide in them. They are gifts given directly to us by God.

Since we are called, a uniquely designed glass home has been crafted for each of us. **God called us to it for the sake of others**. God permits others to see inside. God allows spectators to observe the lives of us leaders on very personal levels. God desires that we yield to Him in every area of our lives so that others may see the immeasurable power of His working in us. God places us in the unique glass house in our neighborhoods so we prove His existence through us. God gives others opportunities to follow our godly example. God gives us a gift by allowing us to be the living example for others.

God called us to live in such a home for our sakes. God hopes that we accept the responsibilities that accompany living in our glass houses. He hopes we follow His requirements for our personal, righteous living. God places us here for our own refinement and purification as leaders. God appoints us to live in glass houses, enabling us to choose the leadership characterized by integrity, sincerity, and transparency. He asks us to live in complete reliance on Him, ensuring our success as a leader. God has given us the gift of an intimate relationship with Him as our Leader, so we may lead others well.

God called us to live in our glass houses for His sake. God filters everything within our glass houses. He receives all glory and honor when others witness our love, obedience, and following of God. Our houses are God's tools with which He accomplishes His plan in our world. Our glass houses display that He has done great things and not we, ourselves. It returns His due praises to Him, alone. Our glass houses are God's gift to Himself, because He loves and has chosen us.

One might debate the right of others to view so many aspects of his leader's life caused by his dwelling in a glass house. Leaders might assume reasons to feel that observation is intrusive, unjustified, and a violation of privacy. Truthfully, there are no grounds for debate.

Leader, please understand. God has chosen us for leadership for **His** reasons, and only **His**. If there are concerns of private matters which should not be seen in the lives of us leaders, God will not allow them to be seen. He will not permit His chosen leaders to be continually open to attacks and harm. He dearly loves us. As our Father, God's first instinct is to protect us. He will not permit others to violate our privacy, take personal liberties against us, nor intrude. If **God** does not want others to view inside our glass homes, then **no one** will!

As leaders, we must thank God each day for His gift of our Home Sweet *Glass* Homes. We must thank Him for the honor of leading. We must appreciate and highly regard those appointed to follow our leadership. We must pray, diligently and daily, that we do everything possible to avoid **messing up** God's plan for leading others. "Dear God, please don't let me ruin this!"

Dear leader, if you have been in the mind-set that your glass house has seemed a curse to you, please reconsider. Understand its priceless value and custom-creation on your behalf. Seek forgiveness for misusing and taking for granted such a remarkable gift from God. Grasp a proper, humble perspective of your leadership. The higher we hold our noses in pride, the better the opportunity to trip and stumble, thus making complete fools of ourselves. Be a courageous leader, and admit your mistakes. Fix them, and follow our Leader whole-heartedly, going forth as you live and lead in your glass home.

Likewise, dear beaten-down leader, if you have felt abused, misused, and taken for granted, please find your strength in God. Remind yourself that He will protect you and your house. Be confident in His plan for you to lead. Be assured of His blessings when you obey, regardless of the outcome or hurt caused by others. Be thankful that

God has your back in all situations and circumstances. Be a courageous leader, and get up. Brush yourself off; heal your wounds, and continue to follow the plan God has for your remarkable life and leadership in your glass home.

What must a leader of complete integrity, sincerity, and transparency do with his glass home of leadership? **Embrace it!** After all, it is our God-made, God-given, God-preserved gift–**my** Home Sweet *Glass* Home!

To contact Kimberly or Dr. D. Neil Suders for personal encouragement, instructional workshops, or inspirational seminars, inquiries can be made at:

Email: kookies4kids@comcast.net
Subject: Home Sweet Glass Home

*K*imberly has served along with her husband, Dr. D. Neil Suders, in Christian ministry and leadership for over thirty years. Through God's guidance and personal experience, Kimberly hopes to encourage the leaders of today, as well as those of the future. She desires to uplift and offer practical support to leaders in any capacity, whether pastors, educators, coaches, students, or business leaders, while compassionately affirming the biblical mandates for ethical, moral, and godly leadership. *Home Sweet Glass Home* is Kimberly's sincere, uncensored, and fully exposed account of her heart and life experiences as a leader. May you be strengthened and encouraged as you read.